Tame the chaos...incre
There are tips in this book the most successful, renowned restaurateurs I've worked with in New York City are applying every day to achieve their top-notch status.

Mr. Dana A. Koteen, *Managing Partner, Restaurant Reason, New York, NY.*

With his management experience in the hospitality industry Mike Walmsley brings a solid background of knowledge to the industry together with practical insights. Mike is also one of our most respected instructors.

Alfredo Vazquez, PhD., *Director, Arbutus College, Vancouver, Canada*

This book is a MUST READ for any owner or manager in the food and beverage industry. Attaining better and higher profits is all about paying attention to details in both the human factor and the numbers side of things. Using this easy to read and execute tip book can only improve the bottom line.

Ken Takeuchi, *Business Advisor, Peter Thomson Centre for Venture Development, School of Business, British Columbia Institute of Technology, Vancouver, Canada*

It's easy to read with good information. The Taps sections are real eye openers of what a manager/owner should be doing on a regular basis.

Ann Foster, *General Manager, BBS Hotels, Baton Rouge, Louisiana*

This was an enjoyable read as it captures our industry as it is today, with staffing, recruitment & retention as a key element to any business success...then the core fundamentals that any hospitality business needs to build a core culture that is back to basics that many have forgotten about. This book covers all the essentials that every staff, manager and owner should have available as a resource for their teams.

Brian Browne, *Food & Beverage, Clubhouse Operations Manager at Swaneset Bay Resort & Country Club. (West Coast Golf Group), Pitt Meadows, Canada*

69 Tips...should be on every food, beverage and accommodations manger's desk top. It has invaluable information that we should all know but often forget or just don't do for one reason or another. Although I have 30 plus years in the Food Service and Accommodations industry, I will have this book with me for daily reference.

Steve Jellie, *Operations Manager, Edmonton, Canada*

Realistic tips to improving your bottom line...this is genius...I will make sure that my management team has a copy handy...

Jean-Marc Levrat, *from the introduction to 69 Tips...*

69 TIPS

FOR BETTER

FOOD & BEVERAGE

PROFIT

MIKE WALMSLEY

ISBN: 978-0-9947252-0-2

Disclaimer: I would like to wish you every good success with your establishment. Please be mindful that these Tips and Taps come out of my own experience and work in the hospitality industry and they should not be viewed as a guarantee to your success or profitability. Only you, your efforts and the efforts of your team can alter the success of your establishment and provide the financial and career success you seek. Only hard work and dedication can help you achieve that. Mike Walmsley and Tips and Taps Press accept no responsibility for the advice in this book being taken or misinterpreted and any effect on your business.

This book is dedicated to my mother, Marianne Walmsley.

Contents

Author's Introduction

As a career, the hospitality industry offers a dynamic, fast-paced environment with often contradictory challenges and realities. The Tips and Taps series of books has been written to address many of the daily challenges and at the same time maintain or enhance profitability.

There is often little support in the hospitality industry for those that direct it and even less support for the entrepreneurs that choose to make their life and career in the food and beverage industry. Overall there are few work environments that offer such strong challenges with often so little profit. The Tips and Taps Series of books has taken shape over many years of my own work, trial and error, training, education, questioning and working with countless gracious people, many of whom have given freely and passionately to the industry they love and call their "profession." I hope you can take some of these ideas to heart and run with them.

When I first started "in the business" there were few resources or books to help develop insights or programs for cost control or maximizing revenue and profitability in food and beverage, and certainly few computers and no Internet to help analyze information or search for answers. Times have changed and so has the industry; a more professional work base, competitive markets and paper-thin profit margins have combined to offer challenges and test our resolve as managers and professionals within the industry.

Some of these tips are simple but not simplistic; they often speak to deeper challenges and are always interconnected. At the end of the day, we must realize the sheer magnitude of what we do and the number of people we affect throughout the course of our business activities. Our staff, customers and suppliers look to us for leadership and our bosses, families and others look to us to turn a profit and make a return on investment. These are your stakeholders.

Overall, I have tried to stay focused on the theme of profit maximization, but not at the expense of those individuals that depend on us. It pays to remember the adage, 'Your success is their success and their success is your success.' When we can focus on all of our stakeholders, it helps us to define our direction in business.

I hope that these tips help you to gain focus and move forward in a positive light and provide you with Today's Action Plan (TAP) to help you utilize the tips and maximize profits for your business.

I would be honored if you would share and send me any of your own tips, suggestions and success stories as well!

Best Regards,
Mike

Introduction

Working in a hotel or a restaurant is a great adventure and working in Food & Beverage is a constant challenge. Every day brings new discoveries. It is a non-stop learning experience. As the owner, operator or manager of an operation, I am sure you love all of these challenges; it is what makes our job so interesting!

I have been working in this industry for more than 20 years and I love it. Today, I own a restaurant in Canada and an international consulting company, and I teach the next generation of leaders in one of the world's best hotel management schools in Switzerland. As a manager and as a teacher, I understand the importance of learning. Without learning, our business will first plateau and then lose customers. In this fast-paced environment, having the right information is key.

Information is all around us and sometimes it is overwhelming. Which website, book, magazine is right? Why is it so complicated to get a simple solution to what looks like a simple problem, before it gets out of control?

So, when someone manages to match the right tip to the problem you are experiencing, without having to go through pages and pages of useless theories, this is a definite breakthrough. And, when these tips and solutions come from one of the most seasoned managers in the industry, it is a real bonus!

I met Mike Walmsley 10 years ago in Vancouver, Canada, when we were both teaching in a local college. At the time, I was new to Canada and Mike became a great mentor to me. Mike is an encyclopedia of information! What I learned from Mike then is still part of my teaching and managing style today.

In this book, Mike has found a way to share his knowledge by breaking down some difficult topics and coming up with simple and realistic tips to improving your bottom line while resolving situations. This is genius and, most importantly, very helpful!

As you will see, this book is really easy to read; it is designed that way. It is also designed to stay in your mind. No big theories here, just simple ways to deal with various situations and improve your bottom line. Every situation is immediately relatable; the tip that comes at the end, however, will sometimes surprise you and intrigue you, and will definitely help you.

This book has so much information that I am now using it as a tool to teach my students. I will also make sure that my management team has a copy handy for when they find themselves in situations with which they are not familiar.

We all strive to improve our business profit or management style: 69 Tips for Food & Beverage Profit will help you in this quest. Life is an experience. I can tell you that you will find some great solutions in this book to help continue your journey.

Jean-Marc Levrat
Lecturer at the Hotel Institute Montreux, Switzerland
Owner of SwissWest Foods Ltd. based in Canada
Owner of the A&W restaurant in Mill Bay, BC, Canada

STAFFING – Is your nose ring for real?

First impressions count and your employees are the public face of your establishment. Grooming standards, performance standards, and morale are all a part of the complex matrix you need to juggle every day; open communications and involving your staff members as much as possible helps to develop a trusting and respectful workplace. Fair treatment and letting staff members know you value their input and contribution goes a long way to helping build a successful team. Successful teams mean successful establishments readily able to reach financial targets and profit.

1 Internal and external recruitment strategies

What does this mean exactly? As a supervisor or hiring manager you need to pay careful attention to the process you use to acquire new talent for your establishment. A recruitment strategy should rely on both internal and external recruiting.

Simply, internal recruiting would be applicants from inside your company and external applicants would come to you via outside sources. Each method of recruitment has its own particular pros and cons, and the overall size of your establishment may also play a role in this process. It's easy to assume that the larger your staff complement, the larger the pool of internal applicants that may be available to you. There are several hotel companies, for example that only consider internal applicants long before they go outside the company and look for external recruits. One of the keys to profitability is having the right staff at the right place at the right time. This is no easy task, which underlines the importance of having effective recruitment strategies that are well laid out and easy for everyone to follow.

Today's Action Plan

Review your recruiting strategies. In the last year, how many positions have you filled with internal applicants and how many were external applicants? Based on whether they were internal or external applicants, consider who you felt performed better for your particular establishment and why. You can even go so far as to create your own chart of pros and cons for internal and external applicants and see how they add up.

2   **Internal recruits**

As we saw in the previous tip (#1), internal applicants are those that come from within our company and can fill job openings quickly. This is often the method used to promote a staff member from one level to another within your company. Like so many aspects of recruitment, this practice comes with its advantages and disadvantages. For many reasons, internal recruits can signify an incredible amount of cost saving that trickles down to your bottom line.

Advantages:

- Improved morale and motivation as employees see opportunities for growth within the company
- Quick access to a group of skilled workers
- Recruits are familiar with all aspects of the company's policies and procedures, reducing the time required to recruit, orient and train a new hire
- Working relationships are already in place, minimizing the impact of introducing a new team member to the group

- In essence, they already "get" who you are as a company

Disadvantages:
- Filling a needed position in one area may leave a gap in another
- May create the potential for "inbreeding" with no new ideas or concepts from the "outside" world
- Some employees may feel passed over and view promotion as something that is given to the friends of managers and supervisors
- Employees may try to exploit the situation, for example their new supervisor might have been their drinking buddy when they were all servers and they may now expect preferential shifts or service oversights to be overlooked based on prior relationships

Today's Action Plan

Offset the disadvantages by developing a simple, transparent application process for all internal applicants. A stipulation may be that an internal employee should have worked with the company for a minimum number of months before they qualify to apply for any positions that are routinely promoted internally. In general terms you would want to wait until at least the probationary period is completed before promoting an employee. Then again, this can depend on the situation and the individuals involved. Just make your process and policies very clear to avoid anything that would appear ambiguous or could be seen as favoritism from within your ranks.

Also make sure to provide the required support by coaching and perhaps mentoring the staff member in their new position. Just because they aren't new to the company, it doesn't mean they will find it easy: the new position may be significantly challenging and require your support at the beginning.

3   External recruits

What are your strategies for recruiting applicants from outside your company? New employees from outside your organization can bring fresh new ideas to your establishment and help you stay up to date. Generally there are a few common sources to consider when you need to bring someone new on board.

Weigh each of these recruitment strategies in turn, as each creates its own challenges and rewards for your establishment.

1. References from current employees, maybe their friends or family (do you offer a "finder's fee" after a new hire completes their probationary period?)
2. Educational programs from schools or colleges with a co-op as part of their school programs
3. Your own network of contacts
4. External advertising in print, via the Internet, or other social media channels

Advantages:

- Brings in new life and energy
- New recruits may bring new ideas about what competitors in the industry are doing
- External recruits may help avoid political problems connected with internal recruits
- New recruits are normally highly motivated to succeed in their new position

Disadvantages:

- External recruits are more expensive
- There is a greater lag period until they are up to speed with performance standards
- It's a time consuming process to advertise, recruit, interview, hire, orient and train
- Internal applicants may feel there is no or a limited future for them if external applicants are frequently sought; this may possibly encourage a higher than normal turnover rate of staff and a reduced sense of employee morale

Today's Action Plan

Review your processes for recruitment and consider what would work best for your establishment. Each company is different when it comes to their HR strategies, and at the same time policies and processes should be followed to enable you to hire the person best suited for the position. One approach may be to post the open position in-house and if no suitable applicants come forward, move to external recruiting. Another matter to consider is whether or not your current recruitment strategies successfully meet the needs of your company. Keep a clear focus on your purpose for hiring and the job being filled, it will help you when the time comes to make the hiring choice.

4   Recruiting new staff online

Very few companies use print advertising anymore to hire new employees. Hiring online is where it's at. You can use online applications to help control the incoming flow of applicants. Do you only want applications by email or will you set up a specific time and date for people to drop off resumes? If you go down this route, you should be the one there to receive the applications, as this will give you the opportunity to meet people face-to-face to get that all-important first impression. First impressions go both ways here. What makes your company an attractive place to work? And what first impression makes that applicant an attractive candidate to consider for employment at your establishment?

Or do you have an employee that doesn't know they are leaving yet? The anonymity of the Internet and online applications can give you the safeguard you need until a suitable candidate can be interviewed and hired. Be careful of what you find in the application pool. If you are posting an anonymous ad, you might be surprised to see an application from a current staff member. It's an unexpected shock when it happens.

Today's Action Plan

Have a look at the positions with the highest turnover rates in your establishment. Write up a short ad for each of these positions. Things to consider: the job title on the job description, the main job activities or tasks that need to be performed on a regular basis, the overall requirements, qualifications and performance standards.

Also keep in mind your local labor standards in terms of the wording in your ads. Another consideration is your company branding. A job ad, even on the Internet, is the same as any other advertising you use for your company: it should reflect your brand in much the same way as your advertising for any other event or promotion.

Some common wording in job ads speaks to the issue of brand identity for both the customer and company employees. Who wouldn't want to apply to these job postings:

"...we know that our remarkable team of 3,000 professionals in nine casinos and three community gaming centers is what makes us stand out..."

"Denny's Restaurants has established itself as an innovative leader in exceeding guest expectations since 1953. With 50 restaurants across Canada and growing, there are plenty of opportunities to experience the best in family dining."

"Our Managers are hands-on and our team works together to deliver the Perfect Guest Experience to our guests each and every time. We genuinely care about each Guest and every Associate that works with us."

5 Have a designated trainer for new hires

As the supervisor or manager, you may not be the best person to do the training for new employees. You want to be involved in the orientation process, but often those that are closest to the actual line work can provide the best on-the-job-training. This also comes with a warning. You want to make sure that your current employees aren't passing on any bad habits in the process. There should be someone designated that is very knowledgeable and patient to assist and guide someone new and work with them during those all-important first few days on the job.

Employees that are better trained and more connected to the job and the team are far more likely to stay at the job for longer periods of time. This equates to better morale and happier employees. Remember the adage: happy staff means happy customers! And we all know that happy customers come back often!

Today's Action Plan

This is a prime opportunity to help a good employee develop into a good supervisor and trainer. Having a dedicated person that can take on the training and mentoring of a new hire is priceless. Pay them a little extra per hour to take on this responsibility and it will pay off in the long run by building a group of loyal staff members and a lower rate of employee turnover.

Do you have someone in your establishment that can fulfil the role as a designated trainer in each area of operations for the front and back of the house? Who do you have that you can start grooming for this position today?

6 Look after new kitchen staff

New part-time cooks have been hired in a rush to help with increased seasonal demands. In the rush, the new cooks haven't been trained correctly on menu content, portion sizes, procedures or even company policies. The unfortunate results: wasted time, over-production, under-production, recipes not followed, inconsistent food quality, wasted food, frustrated kitchen staff and servers. At the end of the line, you've got unhappy customers that are affected by the inconsistences brought about by the lack of training in the kitchen. This can spell disaster on so many different levels and becomes amplified as you roar into the demands of a busy season. Is this an exaggeration or does this describe something close to reality?

Today's Action Plan

If you know that your establishment works within a region that has highly seasonal fluctuations in business, try to plan as far in advance of the busy season as possible. Having set plans in place means that you aren't left scrambling at the last minute to hire new employees to see you through the busy season. Leaving it to the last minute with no clear understanding of what your requirements are means you will have to hire whoever is left over and on short notice: hardly the situation you want to be in if you are expecting to hire the best of the available recruits.

Research your own business cycles and see where the trends are. Are you panic hiring for the front or back of the house? Leaving it to the last minute is almost certain to spell disaster from which there is little hope of recovery.

If this even vaguely resembles your establishment, sit down today with your key managers and supervisors and start to develop a plan for recruiting, interviewing and hiring needed seasonal staff members.

After that, what resources will be put in place to provide orientation and training for your new hires?

7 Check back on new employees

The first few days of a new job can be pretty stressful. Check back often with your new employee to see how they are doing and if they need any assistance or maybe some realignment in their training period. This is a good opportunity for some informal feedback and the chance for the new employee to ask questions or seek clarification on any points that come up from the feedback. It gives you the opportunity to offer additional mentoring or training if it's needed. There should also be a more formal, sit-down meeting where feedback becomes more formalized, and perhaps notes are taken for further reference by you and the new employee.

Today's Action Plan

You should have a written and easy-to-follow process in place to make sure that your follow-up and feedback are relevant and meaningful. Your feedback and instructions should be very clear and specific: comments like, 'Joan, you're doing a great job!' might be nice in your mind, but it isn't very helpful or meaningful to Joan. It's important to develop strong supervisory and communication skills for every encounter with your staff members. An example of more meaningful feedback would have been, 'Joan, you did a great job this evening working on your own, you fit in well with your co-workers and I like the way you handled that potentially problematic guest at table three. Your patience and understanding went a long way to making him a happier customer.' While this is not an example of micro-managing your new employee, it is an example to show her that you are watching her work performance and you are there if she needs you.

Remember, you can allocate the training to one person or even a work team, but you are the one that is ultimately responsible for making sure that your new employee is fitting in and meeting your performance expectations. Take up those opportunities to provide meaningful feedback. Go ahead – who can you give meaningful positive feedback to today?

8 Get into the kitchen!

For many restaurant, bar owners and managers, the kitchen is often uncharted turf; the cloistered domain of the chef and their crew. As an owner or manager you need to know several things to help you manage your chef and manage the kitchen. Many put their complete support and confidence behind their chefs and rightly so: they are well-trained and highly experienced. At the same time, your business should be designed to make you a profit, provide wages to your staff and management and provide a service to your customers. You should make yourself known in the kitchen, visit often and know what goes on there.

As an owner or manager, you have hired your chef for their expertise and experience. That doesn't mean that you should abdicate total responsibility and knowledge about the inner workings of the kitchen; it does mean that you should take an active role with the chef and understand what challenges the kitchen has and what keeps the staff in the back of the house motivated. You should know what's going on, but the kitchen is still the chef's domain: let them manage it with your support, especially if kitchen production isn't your "thing." Above all, resist any temptation you might have to micro-manage your chief or their kitchen.

Today's Action Plan

Schedule time with your chef and spend an hour in the kitchen with them today. Pick a subject; food cost challenges, labor, staff training, suppliers, or even yesterday's soccer game. The point is to be comfortable in the kitchen and to know who the staff members are and be observant of the inner kitchen workings.

Being able to openly communicate with your chef or kitchen manager goes a long way to helping build trust and communication between the front and back of the house, and helps avoid the "us" and "them" attitude that sometimes arises between these two areas. It also goes a long way in establishing a strong supportive rapport should your action or intervention ever be needed in the kitchen.

9 Talk to your dishwashers

Okay, dish washing isn't the most glamorous job on the planet, but it's certainly one of the most essential positions in your establishment for so many reasons. It is also the place that many people get their start in the food and beverage industry, and a good place to help them get off on the right foot. I know two general managers and a food and beverage manager who all got their start washing dishes in five-star hotels. Staying power says something about the tenacity and work ethic of these business leaders. Here is your chance to foster it or kill it within your own ranks. Spend some time in the dish pit: you might be surprised by what you'll learn!

Today's Action Plan

Talk to your dish washer about what their biggest challenges are on the job. What can you do to help make their time at work flow more efficiently?

Also ask them what food items they see as the most commonly left over on customer's plates. This should give you a clue about item selection and portion sizes on your menus and how your guests perceive them. It could also indicate where some of your profits are going if the portion sizes proffered vary from what your recipes are built for.

Go ahead – roll up your sleeves and dive into the dish pit for an hour.

10 Company culture

How can we define a company's culture? The Oxford Dictionary gives us this definition: 'The mode of behavior within a particular group.' This is a good definition on the surface, but it goes much deeper than this. The majority of company or corporate cultures are normally pretty good, but in some cases it can be downright unethical: we only need to think of examples from investment banking in the last few years to see what bad can look like!

Every person is unique and so are companies and organizations. It is thought that there is a general behavioral thread that runs through a company creating a common pattern in how it conducts routine business decisions and activities and the manner in which it engages with staff members and their customers.

Why is this important? Many people at multiple levels are affected by what we have come to call "company culture." This includes things like dress code, hours of work, promotion, employee development and values such as quality, authenticity and honesty, to name only three.

Today's Action Plan

Getting the culture right is by far the most important task for any company. Culture may initially come directly from the CEO, but over time it is made up of the often very diverse composition of the supervisors and employees that work at the company. Because of this, change, particularly cultural change, within a company can be very slow. Recruiting the best people, fair compensation and equity are only a start to helping build a great company culture. A demonstrated passion for your vision as a leader is hugely important. (Oh, and your vision should be on the larger path to the greater good.)

Here are six questions that you might want to ask to see if you can better define the culture at your company:

1. Can you describe your company's current culture?
2. What does a typical workday look like for each of the employees?
3. What are the most important company values?
4. Are these values generally shared by all within the company?
5. How easy is it to communicate between the different levels of your company?

6.   What can you say about the overall work environment?

Certainly there are more questions we could ask ourselves, but these are a start. Answers to these questions should help you better identify company priorities and even future company direction. The best we can hope for as a leader or manager is to create an overall unifying culture and nurture its values and customs amongst employees and customers. It's these shared values and customs that speak the loudest to each of the different stakeholders in our company and also speak volumes about your corporate success or failure. This isn't something that you can change today, but you can start by asking yourself these six questions and refining them to meet the practical needs of your own establishment.

11 Employee retention

Developing some strategies to enhance employee retention may help to reduce employee turnover. Consider
what your employees potentially complain about when
they go home at the end of the day.

- Is it a lack of respect in the workplace?
- Do you offer fair compensation including bene-
  fits?
- What about shared goals and values?
- What about honest effective feedback and the
  ability to effectively listen to employees?
- Is it stress?
- Or does your competitor down the road offer
  higher pay rates or offer what your employees
  might consider as better working conditions?

All of these and more are things that employees routinely complain about, and if they can't satisfy their
needs with one employer, they move on to the next.
This is especially true of top-performing employees.

They know how good they are, and if they perceive that the discomfort of staying with one employer is greater than that of leaving, you have lost them to the competition.

Keep your employees involved in the company; provide them with any information that tells them how they fit into the overall organization of your company and what it means to have them as trusted employees. Be flexible: your company's success is their success and vice versa. Overall, listen to them. Try to maintain open communications with all employees and work to understand what they are about and what motivates them. Remember that not all employees are motivated by the same things and motivation can shift and change over time as well.

Today's Action Plan

Take a step forward and see if you can list five reasons why your employees want to stay with your organization and five reasons why they might want to leave.

Remember to celebrate small and big successes with your employees and maintain an open positive approach to communicating with each of them. It's important to connect with people personally before being able to connect with them professionally, and open communication helps you achieve that. It could be as simple as being able to understand what motivates each of your employees and why. This doesn't mean partying with your employees after work, but it does mean understanding them and what motives or de-motivates them while they are on the job.

A brave move might be to ask your employees those two questions, why do you stay and why might you want to leave? For some this is about moving out of your comfort zone and branching out into uncharted waters, for others this type of conversation with employees might be more natural. Experiment and see what you can learn from your employees. There is little to no gray area here: you will find out some truly amazing things about your company culture and the people that work for you!

12 Retaining new/good staff

Okay, you have successfully recruited and hired them: how do you keep them? First impressions and the first few days on the job go a long way to determining the length of the employment relationship you will have with a new employee. Long before you say, 'You're hired!' several things should be in place to reduce the stress, not only on the new employee but on your current staff as well. What is your orientation and training process? Do you have a policy and procedures manual in place for them to read, and a properly written job description? A "buddy" team member dedicated to working with that new person to get them through those first few critical shifts when everything is so new and raw to them will go a long way to setting the tone of your company's relationship with that new employee.

Today's Action Plan

Start by dusting off your old job descriptions and making sure they are still relevant for the position for which you're hiring. Make sure you have done the same for your policy and training manuals and make sure the trainer is ready to take on that new employee.

Another consideration: Many companies have "Trainee" tags to go along with a new employee's name tag. We all know that new hires take time to be fully productive: give them a break. Customers hate to hear the phrase, 'I'm new here.' A simple glance at a "trainee" name tag helps cut everyone some slack.

The aspect of having a dedicated training buddy is beneficial in so many ways. It is an opportunity to show your trust and respect for the trainer and the new hire. It can help prepare the trainer for eventual promotions within your organization. It's an opportunity to strengthen the morale of the trainer and the work group in general. It is also a good start for the new employee, as they will feel like they are part of the team from day one, and will appreciate your commitment to making them feel welcome in their new work environment.

13 Assess the cost of employee turnover

I could write an entire book on this one topic alone! There are many reasons that employee turnover occurs in the first place, and in general terms these include poor supervision, inadequate compensation and a poor work environment. While many factors are involved in employee turnover, I want to focus on the actual cost of turnover. As you can imagine, there are tangibles and intangibles in this equation.

It's almost instinctive to know that where work groups experience less employee turnover they are more productive than a group with a higher turnover rate. The cost of lost productivity has a direct effect on your establishment. It's difficult to assign a monetary value to the disruption of experienced employees, particularly when they have to interrupt their own work to cover for the new hire, neglecting their own work and the guest while doing so. So yes, guests also feel the strain of employee turnover by experiencing a reduced quality of service.

In the simplest of terms, lost productivity can be broken down into two areas: employee competence and mastery. In the competence stage, orientation and training slow the productivity of the work team; over time the employee gains a mastery of the work and preforms at a higher level, having learnt to handle exceptions and gain increased efficiencies in the workplace. This all takes time and varies from one establishment to another in terms of the available skill level in the labor pool and the actual complexity of the position being filled.

Here are some numbers to consider. For 2013, the Bureau of Labor Statistics in the USA identified an employee turnover rate in the restaurant and accommodation sector at almost 63%, (2012 and 2011 were 61 and 58%)! This is compared to a turnover rate of 42% (in 2013) for all other industries combined: lower than the hospitality industry but still not a very good track record. This 21% difference alone should be enough to send up red flags about employee retention in the hospitality industry.

Some other considerations to keep in mind: over 28% of employees in the (American) restaurant industry are students and work only part-time, in contrast to other sectors of the labor force where only 11% of employees are students. This all means that in an industry like ours that already has significant challenges to maintaining and growing profitability, an unstable or volatile labor force only adds to the complexity. The assumption here, overall, is that other regions and countries potentially experience more or less the same labor challenges.

Some loose numbers used by the Washington State Restaurant Association put some dollar figures to the cost of replacing an employee. Every time a restaurant replaced a front line employee, it costs more than $5,125 (USD) —and for a manager the costs are even scarier, at an estimated $35,964 (USD). Replacement cost, training, productivity, opportunity costs, and under-performance of both the departing and new employee, albeit for very different reasons, contributed to these cost estimates, all costs that the business must swallow. Performance lag is often cited as one of the most costly aspects of employee turnover. These costs escalate especially for a supervisory or management position, where it can take a new hire several months to come up to speed and meet the required performance standards. Some of these costs may mean extra orientation and training as well as more intensive mentoring and coaching.

I promised you some numbers, so let's look at an example. Industry studies peg the cost of turnover as between 27 and 30% of an employee's annual wage. Let's do a simple exercise based on the dollar values we have. If you replaced 5 frontline staff members in the last year, it potentially ate $25,625 from your bottom line. If you had to replace a supervisor or manager as well, it potentially cost you another $36,000.

The biggest take away here should be intuitive. When we understand the value of employee retention and structure our companies' management practices and compensation packages accordingly it can only lead to better profit and at the same time outperform the competition.

Replacement costs are often more complex than what we might realize on the surface and having a clear understanding of want it is exactly that you expect from your new employee is essential, whether they are an hourly paid server or salaried supervisor or even a CEO.

Today's Action Plan

Do the math. How many frontline staff did you replace in the last 12 months? More financially challenging, how many supervisors or managers? This is a sobering exercise but one that is essential to help understand the psychological and financial impact that your business experiences when an employee leaves and a replacement is hired.

14 How to calculate employee turnover

Whether the staff losses involve voluntary or involuntary reasons for leaving your company, it still warrants calculating the employee turnover rate.

Here's a sample calculation. Employee turnover is expressed as a percentage. First you need a period of time, let's say a year. You can calculate your employee turnover rate by dividing the number of employees that left by the number at the beginning of the period.

Here's the example. Your company has 100 employees at the beginning of the year, 12 quit over the course of the year and 10 were laid off because of the shortage of work. Your employee turnover rate would be 12/100 or 12% voluntary and 10/100, 10% involuntary and overall your employee turnover rate would be 22% (22/100). If your company experiences peaks and valleys because of the seasonality of your business, you can also calculate your turnover during these periods to identify any trends. You might want to compare your numbers with similar businesses in your locale to help identify any trends. Comparing year to year, or season to season can also add some depth and perspective as well. Are you within the average or are your turnover rates higher or lower than the average for your region?

Today's Action Plan

Take out your employee files and calculate your employee turnover rate for the last six months and the last twelve and see if it identifies any trends in your business.

When considering the cost of employee turnover and the turnover rate can you draw any inferences from this information that might help you with future placement rates and hiring strategies? At the very least, it might help you to understand the potential financial impact that employee turnover has on your company and help you to develop some strategies for better employee retention.

Here are five tips to help you with retaining your employees:

- Maintain and enhance a professional workplace, leading by example
- Supervise in the way you would like to be supervised; this goes a long way to maintaining company culture and maintaining the golden rule example

- Maintain open channels of communication: remember, it's also about how much you listen rather than speak
- Help your employees to succeed (and in some cases advance) in the workplace
- Maintain and enhance a friendly working environment

15 Keeping kitchen staff

Many reports on the food and beverage industry identify kitchen employees as the ones that have the highest turnover rates. The cost of employee turnover is staggering and there are many ways to address this issue. Offering a fair wage is just one way to help curtail turnover.

You should always assume that everyone in the kitchen is going to find out what the "new hire" is getting paid. Staff members talk, and in the tight-knit communal atmosphere of the kitchen, wage rates become a popular topic among staff members. Don't risk alienating your current kitchen staff members by paying a higher hourly rate to the new hire. Well before you set a higher wage rate for a new employee, you should consider a raise for the faithful staff you already have. You might think this is expensive, but what you should be considering is the alternative: employees want a good working environment and to feel appreciated as well as respected for their efforts, and this includes a fair wage. There is a higher chance of developing poor morale and increased employee turnover when staff members feel under-appreciated. If they feel alienated, you'll find them working for your competition in no time.

Today's Action Plan

Do a cost analysis: what would a higher wage look like compared to the replacement costs of three or four kitchen staff over the next two months? Replacement costs for a line worker can range from about $3,500 to over $5,000 per employee, and even higher depending on the position—that's potentially a $20,000 hit to your bottom line if you had to replace four employees. How much would a modest to a reasonable wage increase cost? I bet it's cheaper!

16 The flexibility of part time

Are part-time employees only committed part time? Regardless of the number of hours they work each week, part-time employees can and should be as committed as any employee in your establishment. I have heard supervisors complain that their part-time staff lacks commitment. They probably don't like my response: I ask them how committed they are to their part-time staff. This is usually accompanied by an awkward silence on their part and I know I've hit a nerve deeper than any dentist doing a root canal.

The challenge is that we want to have all of our employees committed 100% while they are on the job, and that's a fair expectation whether your staff are full- or part-timers. The real challenge lies in keeping ALL employees committed and engaged.

Today's Action Plan

For servers, many incentives are based on targeted monthly sales. Part-timers feel left out because no matter how hard they work while on shift, they will never meet the same level of targeted sales as a full-timer. Make it fair to everyone: rethink your commitment to all servers regardless of whether they are full or part time. Try calculating sales by the hour when employees are on shift. This should give you a truer picture of actual employee performance (in terms of sales) and be easier to measure. By calculating sales by hour per employees you get closer to comparing apples to apples. That way everyone feels included and appreciated for their efforts.

Calculating the sales by hour makes it easier to see which server's average sales have improved overall and makes it easier to measure a winner if that's your goal. Wouldn't it be something to find out that you have part-time servers that actually outshine full-time employees in their hourly sales! Test my theory and calculate it today, and see where opportunities exist to work with your servers to increase sales and help maximize revenue.

17 Best suggestions

Okay, everyone does this, or they should. Offer your staff members the opportunity to provide open (and anonymous?) feedback by offering their best suggestions to reduce costs and waste or ways to enhance the experience your guests have at your establishment. There are great ideas all around us and it pays to tap into our employees to help build brand and customer satisfaction and maybe even reduce costs at the same time. And it can be a great morale booster. When employees feel that their efforts and suggestions are respected and acted upon they feel more engaged in the company and company culture.

Today's Action Plan

Set this up as a competition for the best suggestion as voted by a staff committee. Don't do this all the time, or it gets relegated to routine and interest amongst your staff members will drop off over time. Maybe do it quarterly and make sure you act on the suggestions and give credit where credit is due!

Offer prizes for the best suggestions: a gift certificate to a local spa, or a weekend getaway. Maybe offer a week off with pay and a trip to the new ski resort everyone is talking about. If you are a hotel operation, this can become even easier; as you may offer a reciprocating offer with a hotel in another city or region to host their award-winning staff members and them yours.

18 Staff security: Leaving at the end of a shift

Staff members departing at the end of their work shift should leave by the front door or staff entry/exit. This is important for several reasons, and most importantly for the staff members' safety, as these areas are often monitored by security cameras.

This is for your own security as well: departing staff members should not be leaving with anything "extra" at the end of a shift. Don't put your staff or your establishment at risk by giving them the opportunity to remove items they shouldn't. At the same time employees should feel safe while coming to and leaving from work.

Today's Action Plan

What is your current practice with employees arriving and departing for their shifts? Employees should never be leaving or arriving via the kitchen doors or the receiving dock, as this gives rise to security and safety risks.

Make sure your employees are safe; do you have an escort policy in place where a co-worker, supervisor or a member of your security team can walk an employee out to their vehicle in a dark parking lot late at night? Or even walk with an employee to the local transit stop to make sure they get the bus safely? If you don't currently have a program in place, ask your employees for suggestions that would help make them feel more secure, especially when leaving after a late evening shift.

19 Answer yes or no to contracting out certain jobs

Who likes to clean bathrooms and wash floors at the end of a long working shift? What about cleaning the draft beer lines at 3AM? Not everyone likes to do these jobs at the end of a long night, much less coming in early to do them either. And let's face it; regular staff members may not be very good at some of these jobs anyway. Consider contracting out these jobs to the professionals. You will save in the long run and meet the standards that you set for the frequency and quality of these outsourced jobs. And regular service staff won't complain about having to do this extra work after a long busy shift

Cleanliness also sends a message to your customers and staff members as well. If it's important to you, it will be important to them.

Today's Action Plan

There is no excuse for not keeping things clean, tidy and orderly during working hours, but contract out the bigger cleaning tasks.

Kitchen ventilation systems and related maintenance are good examples of things to outsource to the pros, also having the pros clean and certify their work may help on insurance issues as well.

Washrooms and floors also benefit from professional cleaning and sanitation.

Don't limit the cleaning to the inside: on the outside, sidewalks and parking lots should also be cleaned and free of debris, litter and by all means should be free of cigarette butts as well!

Checking with local health authorities too can help you to develop guidelines for different cleaning requirements that meet required standards. Talk to your insurance providers as well to see how you can save money on your annual insurance premiums by having qualified professional cleaners take on these tasks on a regularly scheduled basis.

What major cleaning jobs are your staff members currently doing as part of their assigned duties? Which of these can be outsourced to the professionals?

This is another area where the professional associations in your locale can help: ask about a preferred supplier list or cleaning companies that are also members of your beverage, hotel or restaurant associations. These suppliers may give preferred rates to association members.

SUPPLIERS – Stakeholders to rely on

Supply chain management has never been more vital to the success of your establishment. Issues of food security and sustainability continue to grow, as do the challenges in crop supplies in an era of global warming. There is no better time than now to have a look at your supply chain and how you manage your purchasing budget. Remember that if you are successful so are your suppliers, and vice versa. There are many stakeholders vested in your success and profitability: make sure you allow your suppliers to be a strong part of your equation for success.

20 Supplier relations

How do you get along with your suppliers? Is your relationship adversarial or co-operative, or somewhere in between? A good supplier is worth more than their weight in gold. Remember, open communication must flow in both directions.

A number of years ago, I took over as corporate purchaser for a mid- to large-sized company. Among other supplier challenges, we were having trouble with our dairy supplier. As the new guy on the block, I meet with the dairy sales rep and his boss on a number of occasions and expressed our need for delivery six days a week and not their predetermined three or four. We were getting too much product at a time and it was difficult to store and control our high turnover rates while managing with a restricted storage space. We went back and forth for about three months with no change. I contacted their competitors, who were more than happy to deliver six days a week and a 7% reduction in price! It worked out to almost $12,000 a year in savings and I had the delivery schedule that met my company's needs, plus the supplier rotated the stock on delivery to maintain FIFO (First in – First Out) and credited us for older potentially dated inventory they took back as returns. It was a winning solution for all but the old supplier! The old supplier's response when we dropped them? 'We didn't realize it was important to you!' WOW, after three months of talking you would have thought they would clue in!

Make sure you keep that communication wide open so that the relationship works in everyone's best interest. Keep asking questions until you get the answers you need. If they aren't forthcoming, maybe it's time to move on to a new supplier.

Today's Action Plan

Not all companies purchase in high volumes; nevertheless it is still a good practice to review your suppliers. How long have you been working with your current suppliers? Are they meeting your needs, (price, specifications, quality and delivery schedule)?

Make a schedule to meet with your suppliers over the next few weeks and have a closer look at what you spend with them and how your communications flow in each direction. Start with your largest, most strategic suppliers first.

Supplier evaluations are something that should be done a few times a year. I would suggest that it's something you would want to do formally every 4 to 6 months with your big suppliers and informally every 2 to 3 months. Regardless of your establishment's size, it really does pay off to have these reviews with your suppliers; after all, they carry as much risk as you do based on your success.

21 Receiving food items from suppliers

Do you have a procedure in place for receiving food shipments from suppliers? Incoming shipments should be checked at your convenience, not the convenience of a hurried driver or delivery person. The manager's appearance on the loading dock during receiving can send a powerful message to all involved in the receiving process, including the delivery person!

Food is your raison d'être. If your food cost is 33% it means that 33 cents out of every dollar goes to product and deserves your attention as much if not more than any other costs in your establishment. Careless receiving practices can lead to far too many problems that negatively affect production in terms of quantity, quality, projected costs and profit.

Today's Action Plan

What is your process? It might be time to review it or to take part in the actual receiving process yourself to monitor activities. Your presence on the receiving dock will certainly be noticed by your receiving staff and the company delivering your products.

Make a quick review of your current receiving practices and see if anything needs to change.

Here are **10 tips** you might want to consider:

- Never accept spoiled, damaged goods or broken cases into your establishment
- Only purchase from approved venders
- Check the temperature of incoming items to make sure they are in the recommended safe temperature zones: post a chart on the wall at the receiving dock for quick reference by all
- Clearly identify the "expiry" or "best before" date on all incoming items
- Check the details to see that they match! (Quantity ordered and price match the purchase order, invoices with correct prices and extensions)
- Never sign a receipt for delivery until you are satisfied with the details and requirements

- Note any and all discrepancies right away and follow up with the supplier immediately if any corrections are needed.
- Make sure you have the driver's signature to identify any returned or rejected items
- Practice FIFO (First in - First out) while storing
- Don't overstock

22 Why check supplier invoices?

Do you get your invoices with the products at the time of delivery or do you receive blind? Whichever practice you use for receiving products, it is essential that you check and reconcile your shipments with the products delivered and the invoices submitted, and the purchase orders if you use them. There have been many less than conscientious suppliers that have added items to the invoices of unsuspecting customers or sent invoices for items never delivered. Don't laugh: it happens all the time! Plus there is the real potential for honest mistakes on invoices, especially hand-written invoices that should be checked and resolved in a timely manner.

Protect yourself and make sure that the items delivered match the items and quantities on the invoice and prices to your purchase orders. Acting quickly protects you and your suppliers' interests and you are able to make any needed corrections at the point of deliver. It's a bit difficult to try to make adjustments or fix problems weeks after you have received and likely used the goods already!

Today's Action Plan

How do you handle suppler orders and delivers? I recommend that all invoices accompany all deliveries. It's much easier and quicker to check the information once for accuracy and then process the invoice. It saves time and money and keeps communications open. Memories get a little fuzzy with time and it's hard to remember the details of an order and invoice weeks down the road should you need to ask any questions.

Even a simple purchase order system will pay for itself several times over and give you the accuracy and accountability you seek, and at the same time make your accounts payable function so much neater, cleaner and quicker. Your current accounting software package may have a purchase order system already built in. It would be a pity to pay for something that you aren't optimizing. Conversely, it's easy enough to use your inventory spreadsheets and repurpose them as purchase order forms, too. This in turn helps you to manage your cash flow more accurately and helps keep you profitable.

23 Invoice prices, quoted prices and quantities delivered

Is there someone looking at your paperwork? Have them compare invoice prices to those quoted from your suppliers as well as the accuracy of the quantity of goods received. Any major discrepancies (in either direction!) should be reported to the supplier and an appropriate correction made. Whether a corrected invoice or a credit for the amount overcharges is issued, it sends a clear message to your suppliers that accuracy is important to you and it should be important to them too. It also helps build a culture of trust between you and your suppliers and opens communications.

It's amazing how many times mistakes can happen on an invoice. Mistakes in price, quantity or sometimes both affect your food cost and ultimately also affect the relationship with your supplier.

Even a computer-generated invoice can have errors. If you disregard these errors, it sends a clear message to your supplier that you don't pay attention, and a less than honest supplier may be tempted to take advantage of the situation by padding their invoices. Whereas everyone in business tries to run a tight ship, there is always one or two out there looking for opportunities to take advantage. It happens more often than you might think!

Today's Action Plan

To avoid suppliers taking advantage or just allowing errors to slip by, make sure you have tighter processes and that purchasing is done with Purchase Order numbers for easy tracking.

There are several methods available for generating PO numbers: you just need to develop one that fits your business model and make sure your suppliers know the importance of quoting the number on all invoices, packing slips and related documents and correspondence. I have gone so far as to tell suppliers that invoices that don't identify a PO number don't get paid. Sounds harsh, but it works!

What is your current process for maintaining and controlling this information? Does it work for you or do you need to revise your processes?

24 Complacent food suppliers

It's a good idea to check around. Over time, suppliers' prices can creep up and service levels can decline. Check out other suppliers on a regular basis to get a better picture of what prices and service levels are available in your area. Are all suppliers' prices increasing or just your current suppliers'? Don't get caught up in fads; do research meaningful solutions that can enhance your profit and provide a better service or product to your guests.

Why do food suppliers become complacent? Here are five reasons

- Poor communication between you and them
- Frequent last-minute orders or changes to orders made by you
- Regular late payment of invoices
- Frequent complaints by you about invoices that are now long overdue

- Your checks are returned to them by the bank for non-sufficient funds

Today's Action Plan

Create a simple strategy to collect price lists from a few suppliers and compare them with your current invoices to see if you can identify any trends. Many suppliers are good about pricing and communicating price changes as a proactive strategy on their part. Some things we know for certain: in the Northern Hemisphere the price of produce increases sometimes seemingly exponentially come winter. Comparing prices between two or three suppliers helps you to decide if the increases are fair across the board or if a single supplier is acting on their own.

Create a quick spreadsheet and track the prices weekly for your top spend items and see what trends you can identify. Don't be afraid to ask questions or challenge suppliers to find better product and better prices: it's part of their job if they want to keep you as a customer.

The food and beverage industry can be highly cyclical and sometimes business doesn't flow as we planned – have an open and honest discussion with your suppliers if you are having any challenges meeting your current accounts payable (A/P) obligations. Things tend to go better when everyone has a heads-up, especially when it comes to having difficulties meeting financial obligations.

25 Single supplier versus multiple suppliers

This is always a highly debatable topic in food service. Let's look at some advantages and disadvantages of both approaches to purchasing to help you decide what option works best for you.

Single supplier

Advantages

- Only one service rep to work with; in theory this encourages closer communications
- Deliveries are easier to plan and so too your receiving staff member(s)
- Ordering is simplified and often done online through the company's website
- Pricing may be set for specific periods of time on some or all products

Disadvantages

- Lacks comparative purchasing strategies, shopping for price and quality are eliminated
- Prices may creep up without you realizing it
- Knowing that they are a single supplier, they may not be as responsive to your requests as you would like
- Since they know there are no competitive bids for your purchasing dollar, they may take your account for granted

Multiple suppliers

Advantages

- Price comparisons
- More leverage for you as suppliers bid to win more of your business
- Wider access to a broader range of prices, quality and products
- Keeps your suppliers' pencils sharp as they strive to keep your business and maintain best pricing
- Suppliers are more inclined to let you know about upcoming specials or promotions

Disadvantages

- Dealing with several supply reps can be time consuming
- Many invoices to process
- Receiving products takes more planning
- May require more training or experience for the person tasked with the purchasing function

A single or exclusive supplier relationship may pay off in some situations. With multiple suppliers, we frequently play one supplier off against the others for the best price, yet at the same time the one-stop-shop may render up some surprising results on a couple of different fronts. With an exclusive supplier deal you may be able to lock in some contract pricing for a predetermined amount of time. This helps to lay the ground work for new or seasonal menu planning and standardization when you know the price will be constant during the length of the contract and your menu run. With an increased spend with one supplier; you may be able to garner better customer service from that one supplier as well.

With multiple suppliers, purchasing becomes much more dynamic as suppliers work to compete for your business based on price, quality and any value-added services they bring to the table.

Today's Action Plan

When is the last time you considered the methodology you use for purchasing?

If you are part of a chain or franchise you may have predetermined suppliers in place with national contracts. If you fall outside of the chains or franchises and work independently, it's important to consider the advantages and disadvantages of having a single supplier or going the route of having multiple suppliers.

Each establishment is unique and what works well for one may not work well for another. To my mind it's a good business practice to continually work on supplier development and evaluate your suppliers on an on-going basis, regardless of which purchasing strategy you use. This helps keep you in tune with where your purchasing dollars are going as well as how well your suppliers are preforming for you.

Do a quick spreadsheet to see how much you currently spend with each supplier every month, and for the year. The results may surprise you and give you the added leverage you need when talking to and evaluating your current suppliers. You can even break it down into categories to further define where you purchasing dollars go.

26 Changing suppliers for the cheapest price may not be the best advice

The cheapest price may not always be the best strategy to pursue. Absolutely, we want to make sure that we are getting the "best" price on the market, but it may not always be the lowest price available or there may well be a similar product that will "do" at a lower price still.

This all goes into the consideration of having the best product at the best price for the job at hand as well as maintaining consistency and standardization.

Today's Action Plan

A thorough understanding of your raw ingredients for your food and beverage menu items goes a long way to developing a strategy to making sure you get the "best-buy" for your restaurant dollars. Suppliers aren't the enemy! They have almost as much as you do resting on your success. A good frank discussion with your supplier about your menus and menu ingredients can also help turn up some potential alternative items that would meet your requirements and at the same time save money and maximize your menu profits. When is the last time you reviewed your menu with your key suppliers?

27 Avoid emergency food purchases from that local grocery store

Alright, we have all been in a bind and had to run to the supermarket to pick up something that we needed in an emergency. It happens, but it should never be a "go-to" strategy for your purchasing habits. This simple practice can help you out when you're in a tight spot, but send your food cost through the roof and your profits down the drain if it becomes a regular habit. It costs you labor, as well. Instead of being in the kitchen working, you now have an employee standing in line at the supermarket waiting to pay for the over-priced items and tote them back to the kitchen. Not such a "super" strategy when profit margins can be super thin.

Today's Action Plan

Reassess your food production requirements and order-ing habits. In most large urban areas, suppliers normally deliver daily and in some cases even twice a day.

Clearly understanding the turnaround on ordering and lead time to delivery will help mitigate these emer-gency practices. If you have a tendency to run short or in the worst case scenario, run out of stock it's time to re-assess a couple of things:

- Is your current supplier the best option amongst your available suppliers for these products?
- Are you running your ordering schedules too tight without the flexibility to respond to chang-es in customer demand?
- Are the items that you seem to be always short on fully represented in the needs of your entire menu?
- Is your supplier in turn always or frequently shorting you on these items on delivery?

Which case best describes your particular challenge? I would start by looking at these four questions and then go from there. Many larger suppliers have online order-ing options within their own websites. Try utilizing this as well: it can at least help, as order verification can tell you really quickly if you will be shorted any items in your delivery. Once you have the answers, your decisions should become clearer.

28 Take care with end-of-month food purchases

Your food sales reps may have monthly sales quotas to meet. Review your current inventory and requirements carefully, as you may be able to strike a deal that realizes a significantly reduced price on a few high-use food items. Don't get carried away and end up with more than 2 or 3 weeks of inventory.

First of all, you need the space to store the additional purchases, and you are tying up storage space and cash with these purchases. The increased carrying costs of extra inventory may not be worth the effort, so analyze it carefully before you get seduced into thinking you got a great deal. Remember that you will also be stuck counting this extra inventory as part of your month end. Having said that, there may be an opportunity to stock up a little and save some money. So would a 15 or a 20% discount work for you? Look at one or two of your highest priced and highest volume inventory items: there might be some gains to be made.

Today's Action Plan

Look at the past performance of some of your more con-sistent or high-moving food items and calculate how quickly they move through your establishment.

The real advantage to this strategy would be to make sure you take delivery of the new items after your month end physical inventories are completed: that way you can allocate the new purchases into the new month and avoid having to count it and avoid an elevated clos-ing inventory value which will in turn mess with your in-ventory turnover rates.

If you are working within a large corporate structure, it might also be a good idea to review your intended strategy with your company's cost accountant to see how to take the best advantage of a purchase like this. Remember, you are potentially tying up large amounts of capital that may well be used by the company in other ways. Also, a larger corporate structure may have a lean inventory plan and dislike an unwarranted buildup of inventory.

Understanding the flow of inventory will help you in analyze the decision-making process with this strategy.

STORAGE – Where is that case of salmon?

Storage, inventory turnover and inventory carrying costs all affect your bottom line. Committing huge sums of money to inventory may not be the best place to park your money. There are far too many risks to inventory while it is in storage. Buy it when you need it, and let the suppliers, not you, assume the risk of storage. Remember: your job is to run a profitable and efficient food and beverage establishment, not bulk up on potentially at risk inventory. Use these tips and taps to help you to manage your storage issues and keep as much of your money as possible in the bank and not tied up in your storeroom.

29 Don't leave perishable foods out of the refrigerator

This might be common sense, but is it? We always want to be ready for a rush and make sure we have enough products prepared and readily available to slide into production as soon as they're needed. But does food need to be sitting out in the main production areas of the kitchen for hours? The kitchen is a busy place, with many people coming and going, often all at once. Shifts change; mini-rushes happen along with slow service periods; not all the information and processes that need to move through your operation may occur as smoothly as you think they should. These are opportunities to be mindful of food handling practices and make sure food is kept at the right temperatures under the right conditions. Sometimes we become desensitized to the actual activities in our work areas - it happens to the best of us when we get busy!

Some things to consider: How many times have you seen perishable food items left out too long in anticipation for a rush that never materializes? As a result, storage and holding temperatures have been compromised and those food items are now on their way to the dumpster. This is a number one hit on your bottom line, a direct attack on your profitability. Even more sinful is not keeping track of waste so that at least it can be accounted for in your monthly food cost calculations. At least track it so you can see the financial impact of the loss and make adjustments to your food handling practices.

Today's Action Plan

Take a walk through your kitchen and productions areas. Slow down: what do you see? Are all food items stored and covered correctly? Is there enough for the expected production needs for the current meal period? Is there extra food lying around uncovered held at incorrect temperatures?

Have staff secure it now and make a note to yourself to make this a training issue with the kitchen managers and staff. It's vital to protect the health of your customers and maximize your profits.

Create a simple system to track food waste to have a better understanding of the negative impact on your profit. At a 30% food cost, every dollar you toss out equals $3.30 in lost sales! If you toss out $150 worth of food each month, that's over $6,000 in lost sales in a year!

30 Check that best before date

This is always a critical issue in food safety and one that requires strict adherence and follow-up. There is nothing worse that working on a special menu item or a banquet menu to find out the food item has come close to its expiration date and potentially compromises product quality and food safety. And don't even think of using stale-dated food products in the staff cafeteria for employee meals: the very last thing you need is kitchen or a hotel full of employees with upset stomachs.

Today's Action Plan

Work with your suppliers and set a minimum best before date as one of your purchasing specifications. There is no need for your suppliers to ever deliver any items that are close to the best before date or expiry dates.

Train staff how to read production dates on grocery items as well. For example, canned and packaged goods have coding on the cases and cans that identify the production dates and lot numbers. These items are generally good for long periods of time, but it pays to check all the same.

This is as much your supplier's responsibility to maintain as it is yours; make sure the supplier is doing their part as well to insure that you are receiving the top quality items that you expect with product specific expiry dates easy to identify.

Providing that storage conditions have been optimal throughout the supply chain, there are many food products that are likely safe to consume after the best before date runs out. This might be okay in your kitchen at home, but there is too much at stake to play with this in a commercial situation. It pays to remember an old adage: 'If in doubt – throw it out!'

Quick Facts from the Canadian Food Inspection Agency (CFIA)

Best Before Date

- The dates must appear on pre-packaged foods that will keep fresh for 90 days or less
- Foods that have a shelf life greater than 90 days are not required to have a "best before" date
- Best before dates do not guarantee product safety, but give information on the freshness and potential shelf-life of the unopened food

Format

- Year, Month, Day
- Months: JA, FE, MR, AL, MA, JN, JL, AU, SE, OC, NO, DE

So for example, a Best Before date of **16NO04** would indicate November 04, 2016 as the recommended best before date. From this example, it's easy to see how this coding could be ambiguous.

http://www.inspection.gc.ca/food/labelling/food-labelling-for-industry/date-markings-and-storage-instructions/eng/1328032988308/1328034259857

31 Be aware of food-borne illnesses

Improper food handling is no joke. It puts hundreds of people at risk every year, employees and customers alike. The media is all too keen to report any serious cases of food-borne illnesses and we have all seen extensive media coverage of incidents where people have died as a result of poisoning from improper food handling.

Health care professionals that deal with food safety issues list ten causes that lead to outbreaks of foodborne illness. In descending order, they are:

1. Improper cooling
2. Excessive advance preparation
3. Contact with an infected person
4. Inadequate reheating for food from hot holding temperatures
5. Improper hot holding temperatures
6. Contaminated raw food or ingredients
7. Unsafe source of food products

8. Use of left overs
9. Cross-contamination
10. Inadequate cooking

These ten improper food handling practices account for over 95% of all outbreaks in the food service industry in North America. The top three rank as follows: improper cooling is the largest single contributor at 30% followed by advance preparation at 17% and an infected person at 13%* meaning that 60% of the potential problems come from the first three items on this list!

*From FOODSAFE Guide, Ministry of Advanced Education Province of British Columbia, Canada

Today's Action Plan

Review your food handling practices today. When was the last time you updated your information regarding improper food handling? Maybe it's time for a refresher seminar on food safety for your staff members and supervisors. Your local health authorities and industry associations should be able to provide you with more detailed information about any potential challenges in your area.

32 The chemistry of cooling

Kitchen food production is often quick and happens in large batches. Kitchen staff should have a keen understanding from their professional training and experience regarding large batch production of food items to make sure that spoilage doesn't occur. Soups and sauces are typically the most vulnerable items, but remember that it's imperative to follow correct holding and storage temperatures to ensure everyone's protection from food-borne illnesses. Many products can spoil easily if not handled and cooled correctly, and at the same time can easily enter into the "Danger Zone" if appropriate temperature controls are abused.

According to most information on food-borne illnesses, improper cooling is identified as the number one cause: 30% of foodborne illness outbreaks are caused by improper cooling. The commonly identified Danger Zone for food is between 4 and 60 degrees Celsius (40 to 140 degrees F.)

Take a look at this website for a detailed breakdown of suggested temperatures and time frames for safe food storage from *Be Food Safe*:

http://befoodsafe.ca/be-food-safe/storage-chart/

Today's Action Plan

A review of food handling practices is always in order. Most if not all local jurisdictions have a number of requirements for food handling safety.

Are your current staff members up to date on the latest food safety practices? A quick check through employee files for food safety training might be due and checking any changes to local requirements can also help.

If you note any gaps in training for your food handling staff, consider sending them for the required or updated training. Food safety seminars are relatively inexpensive and often offered over the course of a day or two at most. This is time and money well spent to protect your staff and customers and certainly your business.

Be sure your food handling employees are fully aware of correct holding temperatures. Check with your local health authorities to receive updated information in your area!

Better still, make food safety training a hiring requirement that all food handlers have completed prior to hiring.

33 Does FIFO live in your kitchen?

Often the daily delivery arrives at the back door and no one is assigned the responsibility to put it away. Is it the dishwasher? The first cook? Or whoever has the time? So it gets tossed into the walk-in fridge or freezer as is and left there.

Not good enough!

Inventory management and turnover is critical for so many reasons. It protects food safety and the integrity of the product, and not least it ensures fresh product for your customers. First-In-First-Out (FIFO) should be common practice in your food service establishment. FIFO helps to maintain the timely flow of inventory and helps make sure there is no build-up of old or stale-dated products in your storage areas.

Items should be labeled and receiving dates clearly identified on all inventory. FIFO should be a policy that is written in stone. When stock just gets stacked in the fridges and freezer, hiding older stock, there is an increased spoilage rate, leading to unnecessary waste. Not using a FIFO rotation means that older stock just gets pushed further and further into the background, making it inaccessible for production. It runs the risk of becoming dead stock (dead stock inventory means items that you currently hold in inventory yet are not part of any current menu).

Today's Action Plan

Go to your nearest stationery store and buy permanent felt markers to clearly mark all incoming food items, even dried goods. The receiving date should be written on cartons and best before dates and expiry dates clearly identified.

Clearly assign this as a responsibility to a specific person or persons tasked with receiving and storing incoming deliveries. It's about maximizing profitability and managing inventory effectively.

While the receiver is writing the receiving date on the cartons, they should record the invoice price on the product as well, as this can help to move the inventory-taking process along a little faster and means that the relevant pricing information is handy instead of having to read through a month's worth of old invoices at inventory time.

34 Rotate that frozen food!

Do you buy frozen foods in large quantities to take advantage of better supplier pricing? If you do, your frozen foods should be rotated in the same manner as any other inventory you carry in your establishment. Never let new stock get placed in front of old inventory. Mark it and get a "receive date" and a "best before" date clearly visible on all frozen food items. Better yet …. do this on all food items!

It's not a good idea to wait until your month end inventory to identify old or slow-moving stock items. Try to get in the habit of checking inventory on a weekly basis and develop a plan as to how to use up older inventory before its best before date, or worse letting it become dead stock. If you have purchased a large quantity to take advantage of a better price, you are now out of pocket and carrying inventory that isn't needed on a daily basis. The sale may look great on your supplier's books, but you're now the one paying the carrying costs of that inventory. On top of that you will be paying for it before you get a chance to use it. It's subject to spoilage, theft, freezer burn and what if your freezer fails overnight?

Most of us live in urban centers where food deliveries happen daily or twice daily! You never need to increase your expenses by carrying too much inventory unless you live in the outback and deliveries are only once or twice a week! Be aware that taste and texture deteriorate over time. And oh: Keep the doors closed. Those plastic curtains still let the cold out and warmer air in.

Industry recommendations for shelf-life for frozen food products (that are correctly wrapped)

At -18 degrees Celsius or 0 degrees Fahrenheit:

- Meat 10-12 months is optimal
- Poultry (chicken, turkey - whole) 12 months
- Poultry (chicken, turkey - pieces) 6 months
- Cooked meat products < 2 months
- Breads/rolls 1-2 months
- Baked goods, pies 1 month
- Seafood/fish 2-6 months
- Clams/oysters/scallops < 1 month

Today's Action Plan

Clearly identify what your frozen food items are in your inventory. How long have they been there? Calculate the dollar value. Now multiple that figure by 3 for argument's sake. This is the amount of potential sales you are missing while this inventory is tied up in your freezer.

For example, if you bought $1,200 worth of inventory to take advantage of a price break and your cost of sales (COS) is 33%, how long will it take you to achieve the $3,600 in sales from the additional inventory you are now carrying? It is worth it?

INVENTORY CONTROL – I saw it last week!

Inventory control is largely about monitoring the flow of your inventory through your establishment. This starts with the inception of a menu item all the way through to the point where a menu item is presented in front of your guests, consumed, and paid for. Making sure your inventory is monitored goes a long way to making sure that your investment is protected and that you are able to maximize productivity and help build a strong and profitable business.

35 Keep a diary

As a manager and business owner, I learnt to do this early on in my career. It is especially important for any food and beverage operation. What you keep in it is up to you. This is a list of the information I kept in my company diary for food and beverage operations:

- Date & day of the week
- Weather conditions
- Peak hours of business
- Number of staff in all areas, kitchen, stewarding, servers in the restaurant and bar...
- Sales numbers for food, liquor, beer, draft beer, wine by meal periods
- Number of meals/customers (covers) served per service period (breakfast, lunch, dinner)
- Any in-house promotions
- Any local events or unusual occurrences nearby

- Any events or incidents that occurred internally that may have affected business in any way
- Any other relevant comments like statutory holidays or a labor dispute that keeps the liquor or beer vendor closed for any period of time or...!

Today's Action Plan

This sounds so obvious, and it proves to be such a valuable tool. Granted, it takes a year to create as you want to go back and examine what happened on a particular day this time last year. This is also a tool that grows in strength when you can add year after year; three years of this information is amazing to have at your fingertips. It helps you to understand the projected flow of business day to day, week to week and month to month. It is also an invaluable resource for developing annual budgets and providing new depth to your information on the scope and flow of business. It also helps to identify any lapses in marketing and provides insights for developing new marketing initiatives.

Go to the stationery store and buy a journal that covers 365 days, and start using it today keeping it front and center on your desk. A digital version is good; a written book is better and easier to reference. Keep it from January to December; it's much easier when you have only one year in one book! Try and convince the chef to do this as well, there will be some crossover of information, but the chef's version will highlight production and inventory issues that are relevant to the kitchen.

36 I have heard of a "Kitchen Bible." What is it, should I have one?

No it isn't a sacred icon waved over the soup pot in anticipation of a superior finished product but it's perhaps equally important! Every kitchen should have a Kitchen Bible that includes at least the following items:

- All menu and "special" menu items, including sauces and mixes
- Detailed and costed menu items
- Detailed recipes and processes for all menu and secondary items
- Photographs of finished menu items, as this shows plate size and consistent food placement as well as what 4 ounces of French fries really look like on a plate
- Preferred and secondary suppliers with sales rep names and relevant phone numbers
- Guidelines for production, consistency and yield

- Shift instructions and tasks for all current and new kitchen staff
- Kitchen policies and procedures
- All kitchen job descriptions
- Orientation and staff training guides

The Kitchen Bible goes a long way to maintaining consistency of each and every menu item, and thus maintains the consistency expected by your customers and the consistency of your food cost. It also eliminates a lot of frustration for staff members, as it's an easy reference for them on every aspect of kitchen operations. You have it all on a computer in your office? Not good enough: an updated printed copy should be available in the chef's office for all to refer to and check to make sure recipes and procedures are followed. An updated copy should also be in the general manager's office.

Today's Action Plan

Some questions:

- Does your chef have a Kitchen Bible?
- When is the last time it was taken off the shelf, reviewed and updated with current practices, menu items, revised recipes and prices?
- How often do new and current kitchen and service staff review the contents?

- Is it up to date with current menu items and old ones removed to file?

If you don't have a Kitchen Bible in place, start one today, beginning with the ten top-selling menu items and related recipes. Build it out from there. Over time, it becomes an incredibly valuable kitchen reference that helps set standards and procedures for all food handlers to follow.

An electronic version is important and so is a print copy for easy reference in the kitchen. This could be a perfect project for a hospitality co-op or work experience student in need of practical industry experience. Not only would it be a job well done, it would be an incredibly insightful portion of the student's education and training.

37 Item standardization: What's in a name?

Use standard names on inventory sheets, order forms, purchase orders, recipe cards, production sheets and every form that you use in the back of the house. Go for item group names and then details afterwards. If you use an Excel spreadsheet or off-the-shelf management software, items tend to sort in alpha order. For example ground beef, sirloin steak and baron of beef would all alpha sort into different areas on your forms and be in different locations on different forms. Simplify matters so items are easier to find on all your forms. Use Beef, Baron; Beef, ground, extra lean; Beef, sirloin.

It's a small thing but goes a long way to standardized groupings, making it easier for everyone that needs to deal with these forms on a regular basis. At inventory time, it can be a common practice to bring in someone, maybe from accounting, to assist with inventory taking. Just having your inventory sheets organized like this will save hours of time and frustration for everyone involved.

Today's Action Plan

This is a convenience and time management issue more than anything else. Have a look at your current forms and see where they can be tidied up to make your life easier. Standardization and consistency are all important to finished menu items and quality of service.

A simple inventory sheet might be organized like this example. This also works well for your order forms and purchase orders. When every form is standardized it saves time and frustration on the part of all those that use these documents on a regular basis, and helps to compare apples to apples instead of some other combination.

Item	Qty	Count	Price	Ext
BEEF BARON	KG	11	8.99	98.89
BEEF BONES (VEAL)	KG			
BEEF FLAT IRON STEAKS	KG			
BEEF FLATS OUTSIDE ROUND	KG			
BEEF GROUND, Extra lean <10% fat	KG			
BEEF PRIME RIB	KG			
BEEF STRIPLOIN	KG			
BEEF STRIPLOIN STEAK CC CDN AA	6 oz			
BEEF TENDERLOIN	KG			
BEEF TOP SIRLOIN AA	KG			

This might not be such an obvious contributor to your profit, but it does save you and others from a lot of frustration and a lot of wasted time. It is about managing your time: and time is money.

38 Standardized recipe cards

Recipe cards should be created in conjunction with any menu development and for each and every item on the menu. Yes, this is a large task and takes some serious time dedication. You might look for a hospitality co-op or practicum student to help with this.

Standardized recipes make sure that production staff make and produce menu items consistently – over and over again. This is the least your customers expect from you. Customers come back again and again because they have had a constantly positive food and service experience at your restaurant. Failing to follow a standardized recipe could mean losing your customers because of failed expectations of consistency. Failed consistency likewise plays havoc with your ability to maintain or grow any revenue maximization strategies. If you own or manage a few establishments with the same name, this standardization is even more important and vital to your success. That Irish Potato Soup on your menu should be exactly the same in each of your restaurants and served in exactly the same way, all the way down to the temperature, garnish and accompaniments and serving vessels.

If your establishment uses fixed or static menus (i.e. menus stay the same for extended periods of time, maybe seasonally or quarterly), there is a strong need to eliminate any leftovers, as they cannot be easily incorporated into any current menu. Standardization helps to curtail this.

Standardized recipes should also identify the accurate cost of the menu item and the financial contribution that item makes to your bottom line.

Remember that standardized recipes are one of the four pillars that help you maintain quality, consistency and reduced cost. The four pillars in order are:

1. Standardized purchasing specifications
2. Standardized recipes
3. Standardized portion control
4. Standardized yields on raw recipe ingredients

Today's Action Plan

There is recipe management software available on the market. This can also be done in-house and a simple spreadsheet can serve the purpose just as well at a cheaper price. It may not give you all the bells and whistles, but it will help you keep track of the basics, and a little know-how with Excel macros can help you standardize your information and requirements to help you analyze where your profit is. I would also recommend including photos where appropriate.

39 Dessert is a piece of cake

Maybe a chocolate cake! Does your chef make your pastries in-house? Are you large enough to have a pastry chef or do you purchase your dessert items from a supplier? Whichever way you do it, make sure there is a method to visually identify what an accurate portion looks like.

Dessert items can be very expensive to make and most dessert recipes call for premium ingredients to ensure a quality finished product. Don't let your staff guess or decide for themselves what a serving portion should look like. An elegant Belgian chocolate torte that was calculated at eight servings should be served as eight servings, not six and not four!

Today's Action Plan

Servers should not be allowed to guess the portion sizes on things like cakes, tortes or other dessert items that need to be portioned. Even ice cream should be accurately measured to ensure consistency.

Visual clues like predetermined lines can help maintain portion control and the desired profitability on these items. If you are purchasing items from an outside supplier, have them mark or pre-portion all servings. Better still, pre-portion pastry items like cake and separate with parchment or wax paper to maximize freshness and maintain prescribed portion sizes. These are options to consider if you find that portion control is a problem or that unprotected portions go stale in your cooler.

Do a separate cost analysis on dessert items to make sure you are reaching potential sales and maximizing your profit. It sounds basic, but I often hear complaints from owners and managers that say that their cakes and desserts don't achieve the anticipated profits they were looking for. It pays to do a quick check to make sure that you're maximizing your profit on these items. Make them easy for your staff to up-sell and make it easy to maintain your desired profit.

40 Taken at par

Food and beverage inventories represent huge investments in time and money. You are tying up enormous amounts of capital in anticipation of selling it in what should be a short amount of time. But what is reasonable?

There is no simple answer to this, as there are many and sometimes seemingly contradictory reasons for what your correct or optimal inventory levels should be. Establishing food and beverage par levels can easily help to maintain inventory levels that you hold at any given time, and at the same time helps make sure that there are enough products for anticipated service levels without being over-stocked.

If you have 10 days of inventory on hand in your storeroom and your restaurant is in an urban center with daily food deliveries, you are carrying too much inventory and have too much capital tied up in unproductive assets that are at risk. On the other hand, if you are a resort or camp operation in an isolated location with food deliveries restricted to once a week, 10 days of inventory might make more sense and give you some breathing space if you need it. If you have only one or two days of inventory on hand, that may be too little to maintain a good business volume and could lead to panic buying at the local supermarket.

So what exactly is a par stock? It is the amount of inventory you have on hand to cover a service period (between deliveries) for each and every product that you use in your restaurant or bar.

So let's say that in a week your bar uses 8 bottles of premium gin. You place and receive a beverage order weekly; therefore you need to have 8 bottles of premium gin in your store room at any given time. An inventory of only 5 bottles in storage would trigger an order of 3 bottles to bring your stock up to par.

Par levels must do two things: one, help you maintain the lowest amount of inventory; and two, maintain your maximum ability to meet consumer demand within your establishment over a given time period.

Par can be changed as needed, and often different items go up and down depending on the seasonality of the product. For example, you might need several bottles of spiced rum throughout the cooler winter months to meet the requirements for special drink menus, yet in the summer you may only use 1 or 2 bottles in a month.

Here are three considerations you might have about inventory levels, par stocks and turnover:

1. In simple terms, increased inventory turnover reduces holding or carrying costs. This means all kinds of things for your business: your insurance costs are lower (less inventory means fewer assets to protect), less space required to store it and less of a chance that the inventory falls risk to damage, theft or simply becoming out of date or dead stock

2. The technical accounting stuff: as long as your revenue from selling these items remains constant, reduced holding costs increase net income and profitability. In short, the lower amount of capital tied up in inventory runs straight to the bottom line and frees up capital for other uses

3. A higher inventory turnover rate also means that you can be responsive to market changes, meaning you are more responsive to customer demands and not burdened with large quantities of dead stock and outdated inventory items that will potentially never sell

Today's Action Plan

Make adjustments accordingly and don't rely on a knee-jerk reaction to overstock and tie up capital needlessly. Do you use this method to control your inventory?

Granted, it is often easier to establish par levels for beverage items than food items; however, it is a goal you should strive for, as a properly managed inventory helps maintain revenue maximization and profitability. I have seen it used very successfully on both food and beverage items.

Some considerations for you about inventory levels, par stocks and turnover:

1. Work on your inventory turnover. Keep an eye on what this means: the space required to store it (should be less); amount of inventory falling risk to damage, theft or simply becoming out of date or dead stock

2. Observe the technical accounting stuff: remember, as long as your revenue from selling these items remains constant, reduced holding costs increase net income and profitability

3. Work on being responsive to market changes. You can do it when your inventory turnover is higher

41 Order forms or purchase orders

Copies of completed order forms or purchase orders should be available at the receiving dock in anticipation of scheduled deliveries. Mistakes on incoming orders regarding quantity, quality and price should be dealt with immediately with the delivery person so corrective actions can be undertaken. Having the relevant information on hand greatly facilitates this process and helps everyone get on with their day. Waiting a few days to contact a supplier over any of these issues makes it harder to correct with the more time it takes to report errors.

Here are some of the details that the receiver should have on hand:

- What the scheduled deliveries are and from which suppliers
- Quantities
- Quality
- Price

This means that it is...

- Easy to tell if orders are complete
- Easy to identify if any items are arriving on a later shipment or if items have been placed on back order or short-shipped
- Easy to see at a glance if all orders from suppliers are complete for the day

Today's Action Plan

From a production perspective, there is nothing more frustrating than heading into a busy night shift and discovering that food items were missed from the delivery earlier in the day. If the Receiver doesn't have the correct information how could they know if the orders for the day are complete or not? Sending someone out to buy the shorted items at the supermarket on short notice is expensive and time-consuming. Avoid any confusion. Review your current receiving practices today. I can almost guarantee that with a good clean process in place for ordering and receiving, stress will decrease and efficiency will increase.

KEEPING TRACK – Details are your friend

Every day we face a seemingly overwhelming array of numbers and data in the food and beverage industry. This detailed information is key to helping you to understand and analyze your establishment. Make sure that the information is relevant and helps you to make the decisions you need to focus on daily. There is often a risk of becoming consumed by the vast quantities of data available to you. Keep focused and keep your eyes on the target of becoming more profitable, if you can keep your eyes focused on your company goals, most other things will fall into place where and when you need them.

42 Food purchases at cost for personal use

This is a big issue for small restaurant operations and can sink your ship before you know it! Some small family-run operations may think of their restaurant as more than a business; after all, it's a family affair. Often, the family will eat in the restaurant, and they may also buy product for the restaurant that makes its way to their table at home. Is it also going home with your staff members?

It's important to understand the negative impact this has on your food cost and kitchen production and profit. If something has been taken from the restaurant, it is no longer available for service to your customers. We know this so why does it happen? If you have financial targets that need to be met, this is one sure way to short circuit those targets, literally eating away at the bottom line. It increases your cost of sales (COS) and decreases your profit. This might sound like an obvious thing, but it is a huge factor in the financial success or failure of many small restaurants.

It is important to keep track and monitor what is eaten by the "family" as well as what is taken home. The other challenge reflects on employees that are not part of the family unit. Are they also permitted to take food items for home consumption? If employees see the owners doing it, they may well think it's alright for them to do it as well.

My advice is to develop a policy: even a simple one is better than nothing. Keep track of what is consumed and taken home so the value of this can be credited to the food cost or at least recognized as a cost of business. This is something that is worth checking in almost every establishment as it can be an issue that is not limited to a small family-owned business but can be prevalent in other, larger establishments as well. I know, I've seen it on more occasions than I ever should!

Today's Action Plan

If this describes your situation, then starting today, keep a list of two things: one, what is made and consumed by staff and owners on site, and two, what is taken home for outside consumption.

Develop a simple plan that meets everyone's needs and keep a strict record so you can credit your food cost with the food consumed at cost for staff and employee meals. This will give you a truer picture of your actual food cost and help you correctly evaluate and track your profitability. Better yet, get rid of the ambiguity and stop the practice altogether.

43

Watch those employee meals:
This goes for managers and owners too!

All too often with so much food around and available in the kitchen it can degenerate to a free-for-all buffet at staff mealtimes. There needs to be a plan in place to manage staff meals so they are accurately accounted for. Every time something is consumed and unaccounted for it affects your cost of sales and distorts the accuracy of your monthly financial statements. Profit margins can often be wafer thin, so every effort should be taken to make sure that the cost of sales on food is as accurate as possible. This will give you a true picture of the financial health of your food operations.

This is true, too, for food and meals consumed by supervisors, managers and owners. A system needs to be in place to maintain accurate accounting for the consumption of their meals as well.

Today's Action Plan

Review your current practices. How do you keep track of this information now?

It's common practice for food service establishments to provide meals to staff members. Some establishments have a set amount of items that staff pay for at the average food cost to cover the expense, others offer free meal items to staff members on meal breaks. Whichever option you use, make sure the appropriate calculations are in place. These meals should be a credit to Food Cost and a debit to Payroll Burden or a similar account.

What about the supervisors, managers and owners? A record of their meals needs to be maintained as well.

Be careful of producing a guest check through your POS system. In this case, the consumed menu items are recorded as revenue and may trigger tax implications and make for some extra work for your bookkeepers and accountant to keep the numbers straight.

In the following example, almost 5% of the food cost is literally eaten by staff members; it represents a potential loss of over $12,000 in sales for the period, or $144,000 in lost sales a year, a significant amount of any establishment's sales. A monthly reconciliation like this can help:

Opening inventory	$25,600.45	
+ Purchases	$32, 130.15	**Food sales**
Closing inventory	($24,896.10)	$87,567.90
Raw cost of sales (COS)	**$32,834.50**	**37.5%**
Adjustments– Staff meals (@cost)	($2,602.50)	
Adjustments– Managers meals (@cost)	($1,456.10)	
Adjusted cost of sales	**$28,775.90**	**32.8%**

44 Stop staff from eating while on duty

Eating on the job isn't acceptable for a few different reasons:

- Not attractive to customers
- Reduced control
- Violates food safety standards
- Distracts coworkers and may encourage social loafing

Today's Action Plan

If your staff members are eating while on duty, it might be time to re-evaluate this practice. Staff should have a dedicated space or area away from the customers and working coworkers so they can relax while on their breaks and have a meal. Physical space and other logistics may make this challenging, but it should be a goal you can work towards.

What can you do today that will help you get closer to that goal and help make staff members and customers feel more comfortable during employee meal breaks?

45 Watch out for over-production and leftovers

I have seen slack in-house policies that allow kitchen staff to take home "left-overs" at the end of the day. This should be a strict no-no for so many different reasons. Let me name a few:

- Food safety issues
- It encourages over-production by kitchen staff
- It becomes uncontrollable
- It breeds a sense of entitlement within the kitchen staff
- Other staff members will see it as preferential treatment and may take home other items from your restaurant
- It's theft
- Your food cost estimates just went out the back door along with your ability to control costs and maximize profit!

Stop this practice at once.

Today's Action Plan

If this is happening in your restaurant, your bottom line is literally being eaten away at an alarming rate. Discontinue this exercise at once. If employees are on break, they should be entitled to a company meal, not doing "take-out" to suit themselves at the end of their working shift! You likely would not allow staff members to remove alcohol in this manner, so why would you allow them to take home food?

46 Stop drinking on the job

The food and beverage industry is often characterized by employees that work hard and play hard. Don't confuse the two. Employees should never be consuming alcoholic beverages before or during their scheduled work shifts. I am actually surprised that I included this tip, but an alarming number of people in the industry don't see this as a problem or challenge!

I have heard some owners suggest that in a more casual atmosphere, bartenders and even service staff having a modest drink with the locals or in a resort location enhanced comradely spirit and helped patrons feel more relaxed. Don't believe this for a second! Many jurisdictions around the world have government-mandated requirements designed to protect staff members, customers and your financial health. A business shut down due to alcohol consumption infractions serves no one: lost wages, lost income and lost brand loyalty are the end result. It also sets a poor example of effective leadership from management.

Service staff and bartenders needn't be consuming beverages on the job in hopes that it will help relax customers and make them feel more at home. That's the job of your frontline training procedures and policies to enhance customer service to a level that exceeds the customer's expectations. Inebriated staff members don't enhance any part of a business, and in fact put you at great personal and financial risk that is upheld by the laws in your province, region or state.

In some instances federal laws also come in to power with regard to the legalities of beverage service. Your local alcohol service regulations may lead to heavy fines or a mandated regulatory closure of your business for a specified period of time, along with other potential legal problems and fines.

Many of the laws around the service of alcohol make you your brother's (and sister's) keeper. Should one of your customers be over-served and leave your establishment (bar, pub, lounge, nightclub, cafe or restaurant) in a less than ideal state to drive and have an accident causing injury or death, the server, the bartender, bar manager and owners can all be held legally responsible.

Today's Action Plan

Many provincial and state governments have guidelines and policies directly related to the control and consumption of alcoholic beverages sold at any establishment within their jurisdiction. They also frequently offer resources and courses to instruct staff in service requirements. Issues of over-service, how to identify an inebriated guest, how to handle them and more are all part of the training. Some of these courses may also be available online. Several trade associations either offer beverage service training or can point you to recognized agencies in your jurisdiction that can help. In many jurisdictions some kind of "serving it right" training course is required for all servers that handle alcoholic beverages as well as required training courses for supervisors and managers.

It's always a good idea to consider updating your staff training in this important area. Things change: if you can't remember the last time you updated your own training in this area, it might be time for you, too.

Make it a plan today to check on all staff members, old and new, regarding this critically important point of service. Make sure everyone is current and up to date regarding the policies, laws and requirements relating to beverage service in your local jurisdiction. I bet none of these agencies condone alcohol consumption while on the job.

47 Maintain productivity standards

Being able to manage employee productivity goes a long way towards being able to control labor costs. Labor cost is just like food cost: there can be elements of waste if it isn't properly controlled. The challenge is being able to determine an acceptable quantity of work performed by a trained employee while working towards prescribed performance standards. This becomes even more challenging because there is no set rule to follow: the performance standards of a particular establishment are unique. If a server can comfortably serve 12 customers per hour in one restaurant, they may only be able to serve 5 or 6 in another, and perhaps 20 or more in a fast food operation. The challenge is finding what works in your particular circumstance and creating your own rule of thumb as it works towards your performance standards.

Let's assume the following scenario. Your restaurant's profits are 6%. Let's further assume that there have been some mistakes in scheduling, and over-staffing has caused an extra $450 in unnecessary labor cost on a weekly basis. So the question is, how much do you need in additional sales to pay for the extra labor costs? The answer is not $450!

Here's why. This extra labor cost must come from your restaurant's profits, and many other things need to be paid for along the way. If you are to maintain a 6% profit, your weekly sales would have to increase by an additional $7,500 per week! The simple math: $450 in additional labor cost divided by your profit of 6% ($450/.06 = $7,500). There are two questions here: What would it take to increase your sales by $7,500 per week to cover this additional labor, and what would it have taken to control that additional $450 in labor in the first place?

Today's Action Plan

Have you experienced a similar scenario in your restaurant where excess labor has eaten into your bottom line? This quick example can be a sobering reminder of how important controlling labor cost can be to your bottom line.

At the very least it's important for you to know how productive your staff members need to be for your particular establishment. How many customers can your service staff look after without being over-worked and stressed out? What are too many servers? With either over-staffing or under-staffing, customer service is affected, and so is productivity, labor cost and your profits.

48 What to do at ten minutes to closing time

On really busy nights we move at hyper speed! We get in a groove and just plow forward. Be careful of this mind-set: this can be an important time to watch for potential over-production and waste.

Its ten minutes to closing time so you won't need to start excessive prep for the rest of the day. Everyone from the line cooks to the servers and bartenders will start making "back-up" to cover that last ditch service period: extra fruit and juices are prepped for the bar, extra pots of coffee made at all the service stations, extra food pulled from freezers and coolers to sit on line in anticipation of last minute orders...

This is where experience comes in. Discourage this practice as much as possible. This last push of over-production puts food items at risk as well as consuming a lot of staff time to put it all away again for the next service period tomorrow. The potential for waste and mis-handling is also compounded as well.

Today's Action Plan

What happens at closing time in your establishment? Do you have a set routine for employees to follow? Is it orderly and does it make sense? Maybe it even needs to be reviewed and possibly updated. Which is it for you?

A clear comprehensive list of closing and shut down procedures should be part of the close of business every day. What happens in your establishment? When is the last time you sat down and had a look at your closing procedures for each of the areas you manage, the kitchen, the bar, and the service areas?

Cash handling can also be crucial at this time of day and is often where most mistakes are made while everyone is in a hurry to get out at the end of a long busy shift. Review these, too.

49 Composting and recycling

It's good for the environment and the socially responsible thing to do. Unfortunately, food production can be inherently wasteful, with large quantities of food waste from the production side and the post-service side that are challenging to deal with. Composting is a logical progression to help control solid food waste, and it's likely cheaper to dispose of as compost than solid waste going to a dump site. Packaging, too, is a huge issue and all attempts should be made to recycle all cardboard and packaging materials.

Today's Action Plan

Learn what your local food safety regulations and by-laws say about composting and recycling. There may well be an established composting program in your area that helps local restaurants take part in composting initiatives to help control the disposal and dumping of solid food waste.

Maybe even consider the possibilities of initiating a food composting program in your city. Taking the lead role in an environmental initiative on this scale can only help the environment and support the community. It also helps set you ahead as a socially and environmentally responsible business.

Displaying this responsibility as a business has become an important component in consumers' desire to support socially and environmentally responsible companies. This falls largely under the lifestyles category for determining the psychographics of your customers.

Look to your staff as well to help channel ideas to a committee dedicated to local environmental improvements.

It is also worth talking to your local business associations as many strive toward business practices with zero waste and a reduced footprint. In one of Canada's largest cities the civic government has mandated composting of all food waste as a requirement. Any food waste that goes into the "regular" garbage program will earn heavy fines for the offending establishment.

Another issue is packaging and cardboard: make sure you're doing your part to recycle all packaging and paper. And here is a consideration as well: insist that your suppliers use recyclable plastic totes and crates that can be returned to the supplier and reused. After all the dairy industry in North America has been doing this for years with milk crates, certainly a huge cost and environmental savings to the industry and the environment. What can you do to get ahead of the curve?

50 Make spot checks: Garbage and recycling

Do you know what is getting thrown away or placed in the garbage and recycling bins at your establishment? It could have a huge impact on your bottom line.

Most staff members are more than honest and up-standing; however there is always a small fraction out there that thinks it is okay to take home over-produced menu items or even over-stocked items. Over the years I have found enough full wine and liquor bottles "mistak-enly" put out with the trash and recycling that I could open another bar! I have also seen scores of recyclable beer bottles and cans removed by street people from areas that were left unlocked and unsecured. This isn't the pretty side of any food and beverage operation, but these are items that have a dollar value and can repre-sent significant amounts of lost money over a year. Any leakage here affects your cash flow.

Today's Action Plan

Okay, roll up your sleeves and get out the heavy duty rubber gloves and go through the garbage! What's in it? Is there excessive waste? Or worse yet, are there any items your staff might be "accidentally" leaving outside for collection on the way home at the end of their shift? Make sure you fill the gaps and eliminate any potential loss in this area. What about cutlery from the dining room? There are lots of times that cutlery ends up in the food garbage bins because it goes unnoticed when tables are cleared and it makes its way into the garbage bin.

Bottles are worth money and should be secure, because they can become an open target for those willing to drag them away and cash them in for their return value. Recycling cans and glass from the bar should be ingrained into the way you operate. Many jurisdictions require a returnable deposit on beer bottles and cans; make sure this is happening in your establishment and that you are getting the return value that you should.

Going through the garbage also sends a powerful message to your staff about how serious you are about the profitability of the restaurant and excessive waste.

Some tips to help with garbage and recycling:

- Use lids on kitchen garbage bins with embedded magnets that collect misdirected cutlery

Tip 50

- A well-lighted and well organized bottle and container recycling area makes it easier to store and sort bottles and cans: keep the area locked
- Have your stewarding team keep recycling sorted and clean
- Assign some of the recycling tasks (especially beer tins and bottles from the bar) to specific bar staff, preliminary sorting should start in the bar
- Make it easy to recycle – then it will be done more often
- Conduct regular checks on your garbage – and be seen to be doing so

RETURN ON INVESTMENT (ROI) – It's always in the numbers

There is no other way to say this: you are in business to make money. I don't think there are many food and beverage operations out there that are run as a charity. A fair return on investment is all we can ask for, but don't get so caught up in all the numbers and the drive for profit alone. Whereas a ROI and profit are important to your reason for being, there are so many other aspects of your business that need to be considered. Start with your stakeholders and consider what's in it for them, as well. They are also a driving force that helps you to move your business forward on a daily basis: don't lose sight of that in the eagerness for profit. Keep focused on your financial goals by all means, and enjoy the passion of the journey!

51 Record food used in the production of drinks in the bar

This point can depend on the depth of the detail you want to track for your actual costs.

If you run an establishment where beverage sales make up 10% or more of your total sales, you should be tracking related food costs to allocate them to their correct cost centers. Once you have established your standardized list of food ingredients, have your bartenders keep track of the food items they use from the kitchen for the bar on a daily basis. Cost this out and at the end of your reporting period (weekly? monthly?), apply the cost to your beverage cost and a credit to your food cost. At the end of the day, you will have the correct cost and credits allocated in the correct departments and able to see a much truer picture of your food cost and your beverage cost.

Likewise, any beverage items that leave the bar for use in food production should also be tracked and calculated. In fact, most chefs or kitchen managers insist on some method of record-keeping to ensure their food cost sticks to budget. In some larger establishments, beverage items that are a regular part of food recipes are issued directly to the kitchen from the beverage storage area. Here, too, remember to "charge" the kitchen (food) for the items they receive for cooking and credit your beverage inventory.

Today's Action Plan

Review your beverage menu and make a list of all the food items that are routinely used in the preparation of drinks and cocktails. Obvious food items to look for are cocktail garnishes and fruit juices, but what else might you be missing?

Don't forget the beverages that go to the kitchen for food production.

Remember that at the end of the day you want to have as much accuracy as possible, comparing "like things": food revenue to food used, beverage revenue to beverage used (liquor, beer, draft, and wine should all be separate as they are all grouped differently in terms of cost potential profit and sales mix).

Put together a quick form or spreadsheet to help track these transferable costs.

52 Staffing your buffet food service

How do you staff your buffet service? There should be staff members dedicated to working the buffet tables to "help" guests with their food selections and choices. Having a staff member there, either someone in fresh kitchen whites or a crisp uniform, helps with portion sizing and also helps reduce the opportunities of guests piling their plates high with food that may or may not get eaten.

Guests should feel well-fed and well-satisfied with their buffet meal, but they can tend to over-portion for themselves, which encourages over consumption, increased waste and higher food costs.

Today's Action Plan

Review your current staffing strategies for buffet service. Do a quick calculation on the labor cost and food cost for your most recent buffets and see what trends you can see between these two numbers. Buffets can help reduce labor cost significantly, but your food costs should not increase by guests over-serving themselves and wasting food, or worse yet, taking food home from the buffet table. By providing staff to assist guests with their food selection in a buffet, guests will feel more appreciated and staff members can help them make selections and answer questions about food items and ingredients.

Once foodservice is over, it's over! Don't let food linger on at the buffet stations after the intended meal time is over. Tea, coffee, desserts, cakes and cheese service might be fine but leaving up a fully intact buffet set-up is wasteful and provides the wrong optics for the guest who might feel that it's acceptable to take home the leftovers. It also means unproductive staff members in the front and back of the house that are waiting around to break down the buffet and get on with other work.

53

Compare the amount of food sold with the amount consumed

This is a key aspect of food production and ensures that you meet food cost targets and maximize revenue. This may be easier said than done.

Here's a practical example from Canada in January. Working for a large chain hotel company, our convention center routinely hosted large events. So here's the deal. At one dinner function, one of the garnishes on the dinner plates was three cherry tomatoes. This was what the menu was designed for and costed at. A couple of overly enthusiastic employees used 4 or 5 tomatoes to 'make it look better.' Well no big deal, it's just a couple of cherry tomatoes. This particular dinner function was for 5,500 people, which meant that at *least* an extra 5,500, probably closer to 8,000 tomatoes were used at a cost of $55 a case in the cold Canadian winter! And at only a 70% yield, meaning, you guessed it, up to 30% waste. The over zealousness of the employees increased costs by over $2,200 on this one occasion alone!

This is just one example where well-meaning staff, or worse, careless employees can have a negative effect on food cost, and in this case more was consumed then what was legitimately sold! Without a process in place to monitor consumption compared to the amount sold, you may be at risk of having a much higher food cost than what you planned, and a much lower profit margin.

Today's Action Plan

Don't let this scenario literally eat away at your profits! Review your menus and the portion sizes allocated to your targeted food cost. At the end of the day, it's all about consistency, and portion control is one part of that.

Do you see any discrepancies in your kitchen? Sometimes staff members feel the portion sizes are too "skimpy" and add on an additional amount to make it look "better." Is this happening to you? It's even worse if they add on additional items in expectation of higher tips!

Spend some time during service a couple of time a week (or more if possible) and watch what comes out of the kitchen. How do your menu specifications compare with what the guest is presented with? This could be a prime time to do a little training. I would even share the financial impact this causes with the staff members so they have a better understanding of the impact they can have on your establishment and your profit.

54 Keep production records

Does the chef keep a record of what the kitchen produces every day? Without it, the chef has no way of referencing how much preparation they need to do each day: this runs the risk of over-production, potential waste and inefficiencies. It may also cause last-minute prep of something "thrown together" in a busy crush period that doesn't meet regular standards or prescribed recipes. A record of production should be implemented that cross references the number of orders with items produced. Keep other details relevant such as special events in the community that day or weather or ...

Today's Action Plan

Review production with your chef and devise a system that works for your kitchen.

Contact your POS (point of sales) developers to see what they have available in their software. Remember, this is computer software we're talking about, and new updates and applications are seemingly created every day, so make sure your system is working to your best advantage and providing the information you need.

What could be worse is learning that you are paying for an application in your POS system that you and the chef aren't taking advantage of. A large coil-bound note book works just as well and gives you and the chef easy reference to the highs and lows of kitchen production and any challenges that need to be revisited.

It's also a good idea to make notes about the weather that day, community events or anything else that you feel may have had a significant impact on business volumes that day. This is very similar to the daily diary that I spoke of previously, but this is the kitchen's version for the chef and other kitchen managers. I worked with a chef at a very large chain resort with 14 different food and beverage outlets; he prized his production records so much that he took them home with him every night after work for safe keeping!

55 Are fixed expenses really fixed?

The standard accounting premise classifies fixed expenses as rent, insurance, depreciation, loan interest, property taxes, and licensing to name a few. Just because they are labeled as fixed, are they really?

Certainly some expenses can't be changed, but there is no reason why you can't renegotiate a better or lower lease rate at renewal time or at a mid-point where your business might be going through a rough patch. Interest on loans may also be adjusted, especially if the local economy has gone a little soft and interest rates are falling. Have a frank discussion with your accountant and banker to see where and how much you can save.

At the beginning stages of a lease negotiation is a great place to set the tone for the life of your lease. If you don't ask you don't know. At the initial stages of working on your lease, see if you can get it stepped over time. Here's the reasoning. Once you take over the premises that will house your establishment, money is flying out of your pockets and leasehold improvements always cost at least 20% more than anticipated. So why pay full rent when you're weeks away from welcoming your first guests? Try something like this example: set the lease rate at 30% of the monthly amount until opening day, then jump it up to 50% or 60% for the first six months after opening and then move on up to the full amount after that. Don't forget that you're building a relationship with your landlord, and they have as much at stake as you do in the success of your business. Any help that you can get at the beginning can accrue over the lifetime of the lease and business.

Also don't be too quick to pay for all the leasehold improvements, either! Your new business may trigger required building improvements to keep it up to local building codes. Find out what's needed and negotiate this out with the landlord. You might be pleasantly surprised to see what they are willing to pay for in building improvements that will benefit you, the landlord, and potentially other tenants as well.

I worked on projects where extensive improvements were needed to meet local fire safety requirements. These were improvements that would out live the terms of the lease. When there is a residual benefit to the landlord and other tenants, it makes sense to have an open discussion with your landlord. In my example, in the end the landlord paid for the required improvements and fire suppression systems for all common areas of the new restaurant. By developing a strong relationship with your landlord, it's easier to establish common goals and share the burden when necessary.

Today's Action Point

Have a look at your current fixed expenses and see where there might be some wiggle room on some of these expenses we often think of as fixed. Interest rates are almost always in flux, and upcoming lease renewals on space or equipment are fair game for re-evaluation and possible renegotiation.

If you have been in business for some time with no claims against your insurance provider, see where your premiums can be reduced as well.

Also talk to your foodservice associations: in many cases associations have preferred service providers that understand your business and give reduced rates to association members on a wide variety of products and services.

The same goes for the credit card fees you pay: many associations get group or preferred rates that can cut your fees in half. It's better in your bank account than theirs! Some of these expenses may seem small or even trivial, but you would be surprised how much they can add up to over time: every little bit helps! Where can it work for your establishment?

56 Yield on produce: It's all about seasonality

Go seasonal, go local!

Produce that is out of season is always more expensive, exhibits diminished quality and decreased yield. Just ask any chef about the cost of a case of romaine lettuce in January in Canada! During the summer you might pay $20 for a case of 36 heads and get a better than 80% yield, yet in January a case of romaine might have only 24 heads, cost $42 and yield 50% or less. Now extrapolate that to your signature Caesar salad that you feature on your lunch and dinner menus. What is the cost per ounce or gram of romaine in January compared to July? Now, how many Caesar salads do you sell in a week? This may sound trivial and if you don't sell many Caesar salads it's not an issue, the issue is realizing the seasonality of any key menu ingredients and how they affect your cost of sales.

Seasonally altered prices and product quality can play havoc on the cost of sales. Gaining an understanding of the impact of one high-selling menu item over another on the cost of sales can really assist you with understanding how food cost fluctuations affect profit margins.

Today's Action Plan

It pays to know how availability and seasonality affect price and quality. In consideration of your customers, you can't charge a huge menu price in January and then reduce the price in July, but you can modulate the price over time. Sure, you end up with a slightly higher cost of sales on this item in January, but why not upsell hot steaming winter chowder at a better cost of sales alongside that Caesar salad and then really upsell the summer menu items like a Caesar salad that have a higher gross profit margin in summer than in winter?

Managing your food cost on a monthly basis is vital to the financial health of your establishment, but don't forget to look at the bigger picture as well. Decisions that you make today certainly affect your food cost this month, and overall your food cost should smooth out over the course of the business quarter and certainly over the year. Keep the long-range perspective, but don't lose sight of the daily activities in the kitchen and their overall accumulative effect.

Pull out some invoices on these more volatilely priced products and do a quick calculation on the cost of sales of that Caesar salad when produce is plentiful and inexpensive compared to a leaner season when the romaine is twice as expensive and at a lower yield. If this was a signature dish where you served over 500 in a week, what impact would this have on your cost of sales and profit?

Sit down and closely review your menu today. How many items do you currently have on your menu that could be altered to take advantage of seasonality and be combined through up-selling with a high-profit margin item?

Call your produce suppliers today and ask them for a produce chart that highlights the high, middle and low seasons of fresh produce supplies in your area. It will help you with menu planning and development as well as potentially challenging periods of supply that would affect your profit.

57 Cost of goods sold: Food and beverage

The sales of food and beverage items have very different influences on your bottom line. At the very least you should have some idea of what your proportions of sales are. For example, does food account for 60% of your sales and beverage 40%? Put another way, what is your sales mix?

Keeping information separate between food and beverage categories is a basic and essential for any kind of meaningful analysis or control to take place. This is part of what makes up your foundations of business management and control. Go one step further than this, since the costs and potential income is so varied: separate your information between food, liquor, wine, beer and draft beer. Only when you have these items separated as far as cost of sales, revenue and profit are concerned will you be able to identify strengths and weaknesses in your strategies for revenue maximization. At the very least, you will now be able to identify any potential problem areas much more quickly by having this information spread out for you.

Today's Action Plan

As a starting point, create a quick spreadsheet and put together something that looks like this example. It will give you a base to build on so you can start to understand how and where your sales figures come from and what's happening in the different categories in your sales mix.

In the example below, you can see that food sales account for more than 63% of sales and beverage almost 37% of your sales. With a little more detail, the sales mix shows that wine accounts for more than 28% of your total sales, but more than 78% of your beverage sales are derived from wine sales alone. This would have a marked influence on your overall beverage costs if your wine menu is costed at an average rate of 50%! Since draft beer and beer in general are not very significant in terms of their impact separately in this example, it might make sense to only offer bottled beer and go for a more exclusive offering by brand. This would reduce the inventory and carrying costs of the relatively slow-moving draft beer. On the other hand, it could be offering a menu option that draws a percentage of your customers and provides the extra revenue that wasn't there in the first place so upsell it. Without analyzing your sales mix, you would never know where exactly your revenue is coming from or what impact is has on your profit margins.

In this example, food accounts for 63.2% of your total sales and beverage 36.8%. Have a close look to see how the sales mix plays out for all of the individual groupings.

Revenue for June 20XX

	Food	Liquor	Wine	Beer	Draft beer	Total sales
	$275,098					$275,098
		$17,567	$125,456	$8,960	$7,983	$159,966
Total sales by group	$275,098	$17,567	$125,456	$8,960	$7,983	$435,064
Sales mix	63.2%	4.0%	28.8%	2.1%	1.8%	100.0%
Bev sales Mix		11.0%	78.4%	5.6%	5.0%	100.0%

These figures become much more meaningful when we look at the beverage sales mix in isolation, where we can see from this example that wine sales is a major contributor to total beverage sales. In this particular example, if your COS on wine is roughly 50%, your overall COS for beverage will be skewed higher because wine accounts for more than 78% of your beverage sales.

58

Assess the financial contribution of a menu item

Your servers are your sales staff: do they understand the financial contribution that each menu item makes to the bottom line? Do you?

What we are talking about here has a little bit to do with menu engineering and a lot to do with understanding the sales mix and the contributing margin of each of your menu items. This is important because your cost of sales (COS) is potentially different for each and every menu item that your serve.

The greatest impact on your COS is directly attributed to the sales mix of each menu item and the overall financial contribution of each of these items. Depending on the type of establishment you run, you might even want to get a handle on this by breaking it down into meal periods. Whether you are using some sophisticated menu software or a good old-fashioned spreadsheet, menu item analysis will go a long way in helping you understand the ins and outs of your menu and where the opportunities are to maximize your profit.

Today's Action Plan

Let's look at a very basic example of this. Which item would you rather sell more of in your restaurant?

Menu item	Menu price	Portion cost	$ Contribution	Cost of Sales
Grilled shrimp appetizer	$10.95	$6.70	$4.25	61.2%
Teriyaki beef with ginger	$11.95	$3.60	$8.35	30.1%
Fresh herb pasta	$8.95	$2.56	$6.39	28.6%
Shrimp Pasta	$15.95	$7.25	$8.70	45.5%

This is an exaggeration to demonstrate how sales mix can impact your overall cost of sales. Let's suppose that most of the sales in your restaurant were based on the items with the highest cost of sales, the two shrimp items. If this were true, would it be the best case scenario to maximize your profit? Since these are also two of the highest priced menu items, they may also make your revenue look higher. This is potentially a dilemma, as your revenue looks higher, but your actual profit is lower due to the higher cost of sales on these two items. Magnify this by the actual quantities sold of each item and you can begin to see how your sales mix unfolds and impacts profit over time.

Take your ten top-selling menu items and put them on a spreadsheet and see what you can discover about the finer points of your menu prices and cost of sales.

So let's play this example out.

If you were to sell exactly 15 of each of our example menu items, which two would be your highest financial contributors?

Answer: the shrimp pasta even with its 45.5% COS would be the biggest financial contributor.

Here's why: 15 sold multiplied by the menu price $15.95 = $239.25. The COS would be $108.75 (15 x $7.25); the difference between them is your raw profit of $130. The second strongest contributor would be the Terri beef at $125.25, followed by the herb pasta at $95.85, and the shrimp appetizer is a distant fourth, contributing only $63.75 to profit. If this example were true, your overall COS would be 42.1%, meaning that on average for every dollar of revenue you take in from this menu and the sales projections for this example, 42.1 cents goes towards the purchase of food. This leaves 57.9 cents of every dollar to pay for labor, rent, utilities, insurance, cleaning and profit. How does this reflect on what your budgeted food cost is for the same period?

Once you begin to understand this concept it really helps you to identify what the potential danger items are on your menu, but also helps you to understand where the opportunities are for revenue maximization and higher volumes of profit.

Have a look at this chart and see how this plays out in this exaggerated example. What would this look like if applied to your top 10 or 15 selling menu items? You might not want to do this every day, but I would recommend sampling this at least once a month to see what the relationship is to the COS on food on your monthly financial statements and its impact on your profit. Which menu items could you start analyzing today?

	Menu price	portion	$ contrib	COS %	qty sold	total $'s	cost	profit
Shrimp appy	$10.95	$6.70	$4.25	61.2%	15	$164.25	$100.50	$63.75
Shrimp Pasta	$15.95	$7.25	$8.70	45.5%	15	$239.25	$108.75	$130.50
Subtotal						$403.50	$209.25	$194.25
Terri beef	$11.95	$3.60	$8.35	30.1%	15	$179.25	$54	$125.25
Herb pasta	$8.95	$2.56	$6.39	28.6%	15	$134.25	$38.40	$95.85
Subtotal						$313.50	$92.40	$221.10
Total						**$717**	**$301.65**	**42.1%**

59

The right product for the right menu item at the right cost

Consider what the final menu item is before purchasing your raw materials. Buying fresh top quality, first pick tomatoes to turn into a sauce isn't likely the best or least expensive way to go. It's an expensive raw product and time-consuming to prepare for a sauce, not to mention suffering from wildly fluctuating cost and quality because of its seasonality. Clear purchasing specifications for canned whole or diced tomato may fit the requirements just as well and at the same time save money on the product and labor and maintain a consistent cost and finished menu item.

What about a fruit coulis for a dessert or beverage item? Why buy fresh (out of season!) produce when frozen will work just as well with year-round availability at a fraction of the cost of fresh? I'm not saying stop using fresh produce: far from it! I'm saying have a look at what the finished menu item will be and see what product best fits your requirements. When you do use fresh, highlight it, feature it and price it accordingly.

Today's Action Plan

Understanding the end use of the food products you buy will go a long way to helping maintain time management in the kitchen, maintain a consistent quality product for your customers and control cost and profitability. A quick review of your raw ingredients and how they are used in your kitchen will help you to understand their usage and if the product is appropriate for its end use in a standardized recipe.

If your menu states that you use fresh tomatoes to create your roasted tomato and red pepper soup, by all means use fresh, but understand the seasonal impact of quality, price and availability of many products. Are your customers prepared to pay the price or would a high quality canned or commercially dried tomato do just as well?

Whichever route you go, make sure you're consistent: it's what your customers expect. Remember, too, that there may be other hidden costs in the production of certain items such as excessive labor, poor yield and fluctuating quality. Can you identify any of your inventory items that would fit this description? Which ones can you change today that would impact both your labor cost and food cost positively and help with profitability?

60   One-hit wonders!

This is always a favorite item for me to look for on a client's menu, especially when it uses expensive one-of-a-kind items. All too often there is an item, maybe two items, on a food menu that calls for ingredients that are not used in any other recipe on the entire menu. Okay, if it's a special, signature dish on your menu that gets a lot of coverage and sells tons, that's one thing. But an item that is rarely sold and has singularly unique items in the recipe that are not used anywhere else on any menu should be dumped.

This one-hit wonder ties up money by carrying seldom-used inventory that is vulnerable to spoilage, potential theft and decreased quality as it ages in the back of the cooler. It also ties up capital in unrealized sales potential. And it ties up important real estate on your menu that could be used to feature or promote items that provide a strong financial contribution to your revenue.

My theory: focus on what you're best at and leave out the obscure extras that don't really provide a positive impact to your daily sales. Simply, don't have things on your menu that you think someone might order one day. It means holding expensive food items in inventory for what amounts to an occasional sale which likely doesn't enhance your customer's dining experience or your bottom line.

Today's Action Plan

Sit down with all of your food menus and with a critical eye review them to see if any of your menu items fit this description. Review the recipes looking for potential problem areas.

If so, check that menu item's financial contribution to your bottom line. How many have you sold of this menu item in the last week or month? How much inventory are you carrying for this one-hit wonder? Has inventory passed its best before date and turned into dead stock? If you got rid of this one item would anyone ever notice?

61 Identify weak menu performers

When you know what the financial contribution is of each of your menu items and which one sells the least, remove that one from your menu. Better still, you can group your menu items by profitability and work on optimizing your profit.

This is one of the key foundations of controlling your menu and maximizing profit. It is also key to engineering your menu. Your menu determines the very success or failure of your food and beverage establishment, and spending some time evaluating your menu and looking at it objectively can help with the menu planning and revenues you expect to generate in your budget.

Today's Action Plan

Group your menu items into items that are top performers: these would be your Olympic gold winners. Place the shining stars in the winners' circle, then you can see the items that demonstrate a ho-hum sales record and the ones that are out-and-out dogs that you want to get rid of.

Can you list your menu items into these groups? Which group holds the most items and why? Go ahead, be ruthless!

Top Performers	Shining Stars
1.	1.
2.	2.
3.	3.
Ho-hum	**Dogs**
1.	1.
2.	2.
3.	3.

62 Employee productivity: Meal service

It's not all about the labor cost as a percentage; productivity comes from a more complex matrix of events that led up to comparing the amount of labor hours used to the number of meals served.

Here's an example:

Jon served 42 guests/meals during his 4-hour lunch shift and Jane served 49 guests/meals during her 4 ½ hour shift—who was more productive?

Let's break it out. For Jon, the number of guests per hour was 10.5, (42/4 = 10.5) and for Jane the number of guests she served per hour was 10.8, (49/4.5 = 10.8).

So what does this really tell us? With this example, it tells us that these two employees function at roughly the same rate of productivity over this one lunch period. Before we close the book and say, "That's it, I know how to calculate employee productivity for my lunch servers," there is more to it than that. Successful food and beverage operations are driven by numbers, ratios, sales figures, labor cost, and on it goes.

In order to be truly meaningful it is important to look at all of your lunchtime servers and calculate these figures for a week. Do it three for four times a year for truly meaningful information. This will give you enough information to understand the normal flow of productivity is in your establishment for the lunch period of business.

Only when all of the employees have been observed and data collected can you start to calculate what your productivity rates should look like. Once you know this, you can start to set standards that will go a long way to help you schedule staff and know how productive they need to be. Be aware that there aren't really any industry standards here: with the incredible amount of diversity and the number of different establishments, it would be difficult to make any assumptions. Even if you owned two or three fast food franchise establishments, your productivity numbers for each would still be different. Restaurant layout, level of staff training and experience, all contribute to a complex mix.

Today's Action Point

Do this for a meal period today, here's what you need to collect for EACH employee:

- The number of guests served by each employee during their shift
- The number of hours the server worked

- From these two numbers you can calculate how many guests the server served per hour
- An added bonus would be notes to help complete the picture.

Remember Jon and Jane? You might have made a comment about Jon's shift that went something like this, "Jon's work was very rushed, did not provide adequate service to all guests, forgot customers' orders, made mistakes on guest checks". Jane, on the other hand, worked a little harder, but you observed that she worked well, during her shift, all guests appeared to be well looked after and satisfied. There were no errors in Jane's work. A week's worth of this information will give you a true picture of what each employee experiences during a shift. Maybe this is a repetitive problem for Jon, or maybe it was an off day for him. A week's worth of data would clear up any questions about his productivity and how his productivity fits into the overall goals of your establishment.

With all this information collected, you can tally it up and see what the average number of guests per hour looks like. Now you can start to make reasonable assumptions about what your expectations should be for your employees, standards can be developed or refined, and you can make reasonably good decisions about scheduling and controlling labor costs. Do this for all of you meal periods. I would also do this a few weeks after a menu change to check your assumptions. Different or new menus with significant changes will have a strong influence on employee productivity and may require re-assessment.

63 A menu pricing calculation

When you use objective pricing strategies for your food menu, a couple of important things happen: 1. the perceived value a customer gets when they pay for a menu item is representative of their dining experience (so if they pay more, they expect more of something, whether that's service, ambience, or something else) and, 2. your profit requirements begin to be met.

With an objective approach, information from your budget helps you translate your requirements into selling prices that will generate the level of revenue you need to generate the profit you need.

However, a couple of things need to be in place for all these elements to work and support each other.

First, standard recipes: including everything all the way down to the garnish on a menu item. Keep in mind that consistency and standardization should be a business mantra for you.

Second, costs: are costs current? Your standard recipe is vital and so, too, is a current and accurately costed menu item based on current costs. Out-of-date data will not work in your favor.

Third, staff: this should be intuitive. High staff turnover in the kitchen means there is a breakdown in many areas, and recipe consistency is just one of them. In order for all these parts to work together in harmony, your standardized recipes must be followed without fail.

Today's Action Point

For the most part a common option for objective menu pricing looks like this:

Using a multiplier

If you know your budgeted food cost and you have an accurate cost for your ingredients you can calculate a potential menu price.

For example if your budgeted food cost is 27%, you need to convert that to a multiplier and use the multiplier to calculate your menu selling price. Have a look at the following example.

1/27 = a multiplier of 3.7

If your total ingredient costs for a menu item is $3.79, multiply your cost by your multiplier to get a menu price.

$3.79 X 3.7 = $14.02: rounding up or down, the potential menu price is $13.95 or $14.95

What this means is that if the cost of the raw ingredients remains the same and the kitchen maintains a tight control on standard recipe production, your projected or budgeted food cost will be met. More to the point, your revenue targets will be met and so will your profit. One of the challenges with this approach is of course that ALL items on your menu will be calculated on a 27% cost of sales (COS). This approach doesn't take into consideration the sales mix, meal periods or potentially high contributing items that are in high demand on your menu.

64   What about draft beer?

Conservative estimates in the beverage industry put inventory loss of draft beer at between 23 to 27%. Many in the industry unfortunately view this as a cost of doing business. It shouldn't be like that.

There is only one way to think of this: lost profit. In many industries, be they manufacturing or production, the loss of 23% of a product by leakage would send up serious red flags. The beverage industry should be seeing red flags too. Let's look at it by the numbers.

Let's assume that a 50 liter keg of draft beer costs you $275 and you use 10 kegs per week of that one product. That's $2,750 of inventory purchase per week. At a 23% loss, that would equal $514 per week of waste or shrinkage, (in this case almost 2 kegs per week!). So in a year you would lose about $26,740 in product alone. Now assume that your Cost of Sales (COS) on draft beer was 33%. This would translate into a loss of over $80,220 in sales a year. Even if your efforts to control draft beer put your loss at only 12%, it would still work out to a loss of over $40,000 a year in revenue. This illustration is only looking at one label of draft: what if you sold 6 different labels? Now imagine that draft beer accounts for more than 50% of your beverage sales mix.

Today's Action Plan

Call your product supplier today and ask them about the programs they have available to maximize the earnings from their product. If they don't have any programs available ask them to refer you to a reliable inventory management company in your area that specializes in draft beer. The gains in revenue maximization will offset any cost.

At the very least, look at installing "counters" to track draft beer usage and re-train bartenders on the specifics of handling draft beer and meeting targets with regard to cost and profit. Here again, your suppliers can help you, as many have training programs in place specifically aimed at how to handle draft beer and how to maximize the yield of each and every keg.

Also remember that draft beer is a fragile product: it suffers from excessive handling when shipped and is equally affected by changes in temperatures. Generally it likes to settle for a few hours after receipt. There is a high degree of loss caused by putting recently received product into service to soon after receiving it. Here again your supplier will be able to help you set up the best possible environment to maximize your yield and profits from draft beer.

65 Using coupons

We have all been there, using discount coupons hoping to bring in more customers and increase sales. When we do the math, it rarely works out the way we expect it to.

Let's say we had a menu item that we sold for $10 and we sold about 100 a day or week. If we discounted that food item by 10% with a coupon promotion of some kind, we would now need to sell 117 of them to see the same profit as when we sold 100 units.

Have a look at this example to see how the numbers play out:

	Before	Discount by	After	
Selling price	$10	10%	$9	$9
Quantity sold	100		100	117
Total Sales	$1,000		$900	$1053
Unit cost	$3		$3	$3
Unit profit	$7		$6	$6
Total cost	$300		$300	$351
Profit	$700		$600	$702

With this example, we can see that of course the unit cost remains the same at $3 but our actual profit margin decreases. That means less money to pay for all those other necessities like rent and labor and oh yes ... profit, too. In this example, we can see that we need to now sell 117 units in order to maintain our same level of profit. Also pay attention to the COS (cost of sales) on this item: it jumps from 30 to 33%!

The effect would be even more profound if we were to use a 25% discount, as this example demonstrates:

	Before	**Discount by**	**After**	
Selling price	$10	**25%**	$7.50	$7.50
Quantity sold	100		100	156
Total Sales	**$1,000**		**$750**	**$1,170**
Unit cost	$3		$3	$3
Unit profit	$7		$4.50	$4.50
Total cost	$300		$300	$468
Profit	**$700**		**$450**	**$702**

Here we can see that at a 25% discount we would now need to sell 156 units just to maintain the same level of profitability as before the discount! And the COS jumps from 30 to 40%.

Still with me? Let's now imagine we applied these discount rates to our entire food menu. It's easy to see that we would be bankrupt in short order with these discount rates. And there is no guarantee that the coupons will actually generate enough additional business to offset the discounts.

Today's Action Plan

As with any marketing initiative, have a clear idea of what it is that you hope to accomplish with a coupon program. Before you commit to any discount programs, put together a quick spreadsheet of your own to evaluate the effect on your restaurant profit. You may rethink the viability of this type of program, and at the very least you will understand the cost implications before you undertake such a program. It may also help you to realign or refocus your marketing strategies.

There are many marketing examples that fit different styles of restaurants and food service establishments. Whichever route you choose, make sure you are going forward with an informed financial decision and an understanding of how a promotional or discount program will impact your ability to maximize revenue. Just make sure that your use of coupons or any other discount program is based on a sound decision based on how the numbers will play out for you. And before you start, make sure you have some kind of measureable tool build into your promotional strategy.

Finally, don't confuse matters: only run one kind of promotional strategy or event at a time.

66 The psychology of discounts

A part of understanding guest spending habits and the psychology of discounts is to understand the demographics and psychographics of your customers. If they are currently customers, will they buy more because of the discount? Maybe. Will the discount drive additional new customers through your doors? Again ... maybe. And finally, will these people still be customers after your promotion has ended? There again ... maybe. I think the lesson here is in two parts.

First, can you clearly identify who your current customers are? This would be the demographic aspect of it: age, income, occupation, gender, education, address. These are often fairly easy to pick out.

Secondly, psychographics: this is much more challenging to identify. It's the root of why customers buy and specifically why they buy from one particular company or brand. From the textbook side of things, psychographics often looks at consumer trends, such as their activities, interests and opinions. Another type of psychographic market segmentation is based on customers' values and lifestyles. These are more challenging to identify than demographics and at the same time strongly influence a consumer's decision to buy or not buy from you.

If you want to use a coupon or discount program to promote more business or a new menu, make sure that you have at least a passing knowledge of what makes customers come through your door in the first place. Is it the food, prices, convenience, a hip atmosphere, sharp, snappy looking service staff, your stance on environmental issues or all of the above?

Today's Action Plan

Are you currently using a coupon strategy to drive customers through your doors? I'll play the devil's advocate with discounts: what if you need to increase staffing to meet the demand of the increased sales of your coupon-discounted menu? It will cost you extra labor without necessarily getting the extra revenue.

Have a careful look at your establishment and see if you can identify any demographic or psychographic profiles that pertain to your customers. See if you can define who your "ideal" customers are. Put it into words: "Our ideal customers are _____." These are the people you should be marketing to. Are they coupon shoppers? Only you know. This should help you create the kind of advertising and promotions that speak directly to your customers. Gathering a few new loyal customers along the way is also certainly a bonus!

If your customers fit the values and lifestyles market segment (which we all do, by the way, just with different values and different lifestyles), do your restaurant's values mesh with your customers' or potential customers' values and lifestyles? Are these values also expressed by your staff members?

It pays to remember that keeping your loyal and regular customers happy is so much easier than trying to appeal to new customers that have never been to your establishment. I am not saying you shouldn't be going out there and getting them; just remember that they can be harder to attract and keep! Remember, you can't be all things to all people, and trying to be will give you no end of frustration and lead to the ultimate failure of your business. Know your market and go after it, serve it well and it will serve you in return.

67 The power of up-selling

Let's imagine that you do 75 dinner covers every night of the week. That makes 525 covers per week. Let's also imagine that your well-trained employees, your top performers, up-sell 75% of the time during the week. Now we are talking about 394 (525 X 75%) covers each week. Let's further guess that these servers are *really* good and manage to increase the sales on each of these covers by $2.50. That would mean an extra $985 in revenue per week, or $51,220 in a year!

Now, let's make some further assumptions to show the power of up-selling. If we were to assume a profit ratio of 5% of total revenue: by how much would we have to increase our sales in order to increase our profit by $51,220 per year? The answer is $1,024,400, or, if you like, $1,024,400 X 5% = $51,220. Sure, you have to pay food cost and a small portion of labor within the $51,000, but most of this amount drops directly to the bottom line, a much more achievable goal through upselling then increasing sales by over a $1 million a year by other marketing and advertising methods!

Today's Action Plan

Make a plan today and start training your servers this week on the skills of up-selling and suggestive selling. What kind of an impact would this have on your establishment if your servers were able to up-sell and increase the average cover spend by only one dollar for each of your customers? What would the impact be to your bottom line? And let's not forget that a higher guest check usually results in higher tips for the servers too: a win-win-win. Your sales increase for little expense, the customers have a chance to have a more complete experience and maybe try something new and the server's tips increase.

Some tips for up-selling and suggestive selling:

- Servers need to be authentic and enthusiastic. If they say a dish or beverage is their favorite, it should be
- Suggest favorite items from the food and drink menus
- Suggest something a little unusual: people like to try new things from a menu, something they wouldn't normally have or cook at home

- Ask questions: are guests in a hurry, with only time for a quick bite and a drink before a movie, or are they looking for a longer, more relaxed, meal experience. Their answers will help the server plan out the dining experience and look for opportunities to effectively upsell the menu

- Offer alternatives: 'Would you like <<name brand>> vodka for your vodka and tonic?' or. 'Our home-made chocolate cheese cake is delicious with our orange spiced whip cream…'

- Use describing words to paint mental pictures of your menu items whenever possible

- As with any marketing efforts, always ask for the sale. After a server makes a suggestion from the menu, ask the guest if they would like to try it. Develop a selling attitude without coming across as such.

Try some of these suggestions for a month, mix them up and see what effect they have on maximizing your profit. Don't forget to establish a starting benchmark so you have something valid to compare your new results with.

68 Outsourced payroll

How do you handle your payroll now? For many managers, payroll accounting is not their forte and it's certainly beyond most managers comfort zone. On top of that come all the required government deductions and reporting that need to be 100% accurate all the time. This is certainly something that you should seriously consider outsourcing if you don't already. There are so many companies out there that do this well and at a favorable price for their services.

Payroll is so important on so many different levels and having a payroll company take over this function offers you so much relief knowing that your payroll and all related reports are processed on time with 100% accuracy all the time. When is the last time you needed to manually calculate a record of employment so an employee could apply for government benefits ...? See, just the thought of looking up all that information and making all those calculations is well worth a payroll service provider. And it frees your time to do other things that you're really good at doing.

Today's Action Plan

Your payroll company processes the hours you supply and employees get pay checks. Better yet, get it set up as direct deposits, and then the whole system is automated.

But what payroll reports are you getting back from your service provider? Do they supply the detailed information you need to produce your own quick weekly labor reports by department? Talk to your provider and get them to set up the reports you need by department or category. Remember to measure like things: kitchen payroll compared to food revenue, beverage staff to bar sales.

You haven't set this up yet? Check with your local restaurant or beverage associations: most have a pre-selected payroll company they can suggest that offers favorable rates to association members.

69 Money doesn't always fix the problem (reducing employee turnover)

Higher compensation (wages) is not the only way to reduce turnover and increase employee morale. Tossing money at a problem is not likely to fix it, at least not in the long-term. There are other things at play that need to be addressed, and higher wages will only work so long before staff members move on.

When employees are receiving a fair wage in the first place, other strategies can be used to help reduce employee turnover and build a strong team.

Turnover and low morale are challenges in many industries but seem to be chronic in the hospitality sector. Fortunately there are strategies we can use to improve retention and help increase morale, or at the very least help it from becoming chronic and more problematic.

Here are some areas to consider. They aren't in any particular order, as I believe they are all vital. Having said that, if there was one thing that I would put above all others, it's communication.

Today's Action Plan

Here are some areas to watch out for in avoiding and reducing employee turnover:

- On-going and open communication
- A professional workplace where employees feel safe and respected and happy to work in
- Continuous training that is done correctly: remember that bad training can be worse than no training! There's no point in hiring for attitude if successful continuous training is missing
- Create and offer an open, friendly workplace: it might sound trite, but do you have an open door policy in place that staff feel comfortable with?
- Help employees succeed in their work and careers: this builds confidence and an enhanced knowledge base in your employees and in your establishment. Don't create a "brain-drain" scenario in your company; your competition will be glad to pick up your top performers!

- Always pursue continuous service, product and system improvements, never rest on where you are today, and always strive to be better tomorrow.

A significant investment is required to recruit, train and supervise all of your staff members. Hopefully, as a direct result of a well thought-out recruitment and hiring program, your employees will gain knowledge, skills and work experience and choose to stay and contribute this knowledge base to their own success as well as the success of the company. It's always worth the extra effort to get it right from the beginning and lay the seeds for your employees to perform successfully within your establishment. If you can put this effort into your employees from the beginning, they will in turn, put the effort into making you more successful as well.

Conclusion

The ideas and concepts expressed in this book are written in a commonsense manner which I hope helps to demonstrate the importance of caring for your business.

Some of the concepts here may seem simple and almost elementary in their tone, but make no mistake about it, having a firm handle on the daily activities of your food and beverage establishment helps to pave the way to achieving better profitability and financial success.

Too often I have heard business owners struggle with profitability: they say, "The bills are paid, the staff got their pay checks, I'll just live on what's left." I am here to tell you that it doesn't have to be like that. Start the process from the other direction, ask yourself what you need as a reasonable wage to support yourself and then work the plan backwards from there. It is really the only way that you will achieve the financial success you seek.

I hope that in some small way you have been able to take some of the ideas and concepts portrayed in this book and use them to your advantage.

I would love to hear your own success stories and know that you have been able to become more profitable by putting some of these Tips and Taps to work for you.

This is the first book in the series from Tips & Taps Press and I would be delighted to hear from you and welcome any of the tips that you have developed or used to help your business grow and develop.

Thank you and I wish you every success!

Mike

Stay connected! Learn more about new releases as they become available. Please sign up for my free newsletter at my Author's website; www.mikewalmsley.net

Connect with me on LinkedIn:
www.ca.linkedin.com/in/mwalmsley

Email: mike@mikewalmsley.net

Acknowledgements

I would like to extend a special thanks to everyone that has helped make this book a reality.

Until I started to write my own books I never fully grasped the enormity of the help, support and commitment that others make towards the success of the finished book. In this regard, it is very much a team effort! My gratitude goes out to the following people for their time, support and expertise of which they gave so freely.

Thanks to my editor, Liz Dexter at Libro Editing, and the many friends and colleagues that freely offered their comments and feedback on all aspects of this book project.

Special thanks go to Oktay Kesebi for his insights and marketing expertise.

Many thanks to Ken Takeuchi at British Columbia Institute of Technology, and my life-long friends Sue Tice and Diana van Eyk for their unwavering support and honest advice and comments about all things related to this book and the development of this series, and to so many others that provided help and feedback along the way.

A special thanks to Liana Moisescu for her cover design and Dean Fetzer for his expertise with the interior design and layout for the book.

My heartfelt thanks to each and every one of you.

Mike

About the Author

Mike has spent more than 20 years in the hospitality industry, working from the Pacific to the Atlantic coast for major hotel chains and independent establishments in Canada. Mike has also enjoyed an international career in education, training, supporting and developing future industry leaders from around the world.

As a lifelong learner, Mike has recently completed a Master's of Education degree dedicated to program design and development and continues to work on areas of professional development related to education and industry knowledge.

Mike has recently been appointed as an instructor and business advisor for the *Peter Thomson Centre for Venture Development, School of Business* at the *British Columbia Institute of Technology* in Vancouver, Canada.

Please join him!

Web: www.mikewalmsley.net
Email: mike@mikewalmsley.net
LinkedIn: www.ca.linkedin.com/in/mwalmsley

53361147R00120

Made in the USA
Charleston, SC
11 March 2016